BY THE AUTHOR

Poetry

The Plain People
Between Root and Sky
The Maidenhair Tree
Ships in Bottles
Walking to Santiago
The Road to the Gunpowder House
Other Rooms (Selected Poems)
Some Letters Never Sent
On Keeping Company With Mrs Woolf
A Northumbrian Book of Hours

Translations

Euripides, The Bacchae
Euripides, The Trojan Women
Euripides, The Helen
Homer, The Bending of the Bow
Jules Supervielle, The Fable of the World
The Dream of the Rood

Criticism

Norman Nicholson
Christopher Smart
George Herbert (co-written with Natasha Curry)
Alexander Pope
Six Eighteenth-century Poets
William Cowper: a Revaluation
William Shenstone: Landscape Gardener and Poet
Samuel Johnson: Writer

Topography

The Cumberland Coast

HORACE WALPOLE

HORACE WALPOLE

NEIL CURRY

Greenwich Exchange
London

Greenwich Exchange, London

First published in Great Britain in 2023
All rights reserved

Horace Walpole
© Neil Curry, 2023

This book is sold subject to the conditions that it shall not, by way of trade or otherwise, be lent, resold, hired out or otherwise circulated without the publisher's prior consent in any form of binding or cover other than that in which it is published and without a similar condition including this condition being imposed on the subsequent purchaser.

Printed and bound by imprintdigital.com
Cover design by December Publications
Tel: 07951511275

Greenwich Exchange Website: www.greenex.co.uk

Cataloguing in Publication Data is available
from the British Library

ISBN: 978-1-910996-??-?

CONTENTS

1	Early Days	*9*
2	Grand Tour	*20*
3	Houghton Hall	*39*
4	Strawberry Hill	*56*
5	Reconciliation	*81*
6	The Strawberry-Hill Press	*102*
7	The Garden	*128*
8	The Politician	*143*
9	Gothic Tales	*164*
10	The Essayist	*193*
11	The Thomas Chatterton Affair	*213*
12	The Letter-Writer	*223*
13	Ariel the Sprite	*248*
	Bibliography	
	Index	

1
EARLY DAYS

HORACE WALPOLE WAS THE YOUNGEST SON of Sir Robert Walpole, England's first Prime Minister. Or was he?

Doubts have arisen in part from the fact that there was an eleven year age gap between him and his youngest sibling, Edward, and during those eleven years his parents' marriage could not have been called a *stable* one on either side. By 1722 Sir Robert was living openly both at Richmond and at Houghton Hall with his rich and beautiful mistress, Maria Skerrett and in 1725 she bore him a daughter, also called Maria. Added to this was the obvious fact that in appearance and temperament Horace was so unlike any other member of the extended Walpole family. For the most part they were a tough, out-going, hard-drinking, beefy bunch. To see the difference, one has only to look at any portrait of Sir Robert and then put alongside it Eckhart's portrayal of Horace: a thoughtful and sensitive young man, tall and slim with something decidedly effeminate about him. It would certainly look to be open to question, and yet the first written record of any such doubts does not occur until 1833, and then in a letter written by Thomas Creevey in which he says, 'I never knew before that Horace was not the son of Sir Robert Walpole, but of a Lord Hervey and that Sir Robert knew it and shewed that he did.' He had been told this by Lord Holland, who at that time still had in his possession a vast collection of Horace's letters and papers entrusted to him by Lord Waldegrave, one of Horace's nephews, so although it is only hearsay, it is not without provenance.

From hearsay we turn to gossip, which Lady Louisa Stuart heard from her grandmother, Lady Mary Wortley Montagu, and which in 1837 she recounted in the introduction of a collection of her letters.

> In short, Horace Walpole was generally supposed to be the son of Carr, Lord Hervey, and Sir Robert not to be ignorant of it. One striking circumstance was visible to the naked eye; no beings in human shape could resemble each other less than the two passing for father and son, and while their reverse of personal likeness provoked a malicious whisper, Sir Robert's marked neglect of Horace in his infancy tended to confirm it.

This Hervey is not the Lord Hervey/Sporus whom Alexander Pope pilloried so brilliantly and viciously in his 'Epistle to Dr Arbuthnot':

> Fop at the Toilet, Flatt'rer at the Board,
> Now trips a Lady, now struts a Lord.

Carr, Lord Hervey, was Sporus's half-brother, but as T.H. White puts it in his *Age of Scandal,* all the Herveys 'were at least peculiar', noting 'the effeminate appearance, the eccentric behaviour and cultured occupations of this unusual brood.'

But Lady Mary had grown into a resentful old woman who had earlier been a close friend of Maria Skerrett and had frequently been at odds with Horace's mother. Her 'evidence', such as it is, comes years after the events and there is nothing else to support it. Had there been any substance to it, it is highly unlikely that it would have provoked no more than a 'malicious whisper'. There were enough satirists around at that time to have delighted in it. Sir Robert and Horace both had their share of political enemies and there are few more malicious enemies than that. Counter to this gossip, it has been observed that there is a striking resemblance between Horace and Sir Robert's illegitimate daughter, Maria. Different mothers, but both certainly had the same father. Also, what does not seem to have been considered is that Horace had inherited the delicate features of his mother.

Lady Mary's contention that Sir Robert showed 'marked neglect of Horace' hardly squares with Horace's reference to himself as 'the youngest and favourite child' in a review of his life which he wrote to his close friend Horace Mann in 1785, nor with the sinecures his father bestowed upon him – sinecures with such delightful sounding titles as Usher of the Exchequer, Inspector of Imports, Comptroller of the Pipe, Clerk of the Estates, and offices which assured him of some £4,000 a year for life without having to lift a finger to earn it.

No, Horace Walpole, one can safely say, was the youngest son of Sir Robert Walpole, England's first Prime Minister. When he fell from power it was Horace who spoke up for him in the House and who went to stay with him in Houghton – not a place he particularly liked – when his fair-weather political friends were deserting him. And when he was 62 he wrote, again to Horace

Mann, 'My father is ever before my eyes – not to attempt to imitate him, for I have none of his matchless wisdom, or unsullied virtues, or heroic firmness.'

***

Sir Robert had been educated at Eton and King's College Cambridge and Horace followed in his footsteps. When he started at Eton in April 1727 he was still only nine years old, but this does not seem to have been unusual as Thomas Gray had been only eight when he began there two years earlier. How such a bookish and rather weedy child survived Eton at all is something of a puzzle, but he not only survived, he thrived. His first tutor was Henry Bland, the son of the headmaster, a gentle and aptly-named, scholarly man under whose leadership the school had flourished. But in 1728, Dr Bland was succeeded by his son-in-law, one William George, who has been described as 'foolish, proud, ill-mannerly and brutal.' His brutality was such that his pupils staged a rebellion in 1729, reducing the school to a 'state of anarchy'. This was unprecedented; nevertheless he stayed in his post for another four years, during which time pupil numbers, unsurprisingly, fell.

Floggings of course were an accepted feature of school life. Unforgettable is Lytton Strachey's summing up of the career of the notorious Eton head *Flogger Keate*: ' ... the savage ritual of the whipping-block would remind a batch of whimpering children that, though sins against man and God might be forgiven them, a false quantity could only be expiated in tears and blood.' There were fights too. As Horace recalled in a 1736 letter of reminiscences to George Montagu, a fellow Old Etonian, noted for his charm and indolence, 'I was sometimes troubled with a rough creature or two from the plough.' Ayers Plough was a nearby farm, but the Etonians seem to have been quite happy to dish out their share of trouble. Horace seems to have managed to keep himself safely apart from most of this however, and from organised games too: 'I can't say I am sorry I was never quite a schoolboy; an expedition against bargemen, or a match at cricket may be very pretty things to recollect; but thank my stars, I can remember things that are very near as pretty.'

Safely apart, but never lonely, these really were some of the happiest days of his life, so much so that when he heard that Gray had been back in the vicinity of Eton but had not gone there he found it incredible. Yet Gray himself was later to celebrate his own schooldays in a poem 'On a Distant Prospect of Eton College':

> Ah, happy hills, ah pleasing shades,
> Ah, fields beloved in vain,
> Where once my careless childhood strayed
> A stranger yet to pain.

What made these days so happy for them were the friendships founded there, some of which were to last a lifetime.

The letter of May 1736 to George Montagu ends, 'One of the most agreeable consequences I can recollect is the Triumvirate composed of yourself, Charles and Your sincere friend.' Charles was Charles Lyttelton who became Bishop of Carlisle and President of the Society of Antiquaries, the satisfyingly unremarkable achievements of an unremarkable man.

George Montagu himself, apart from being Deputy Ranger of Rockingham Forest, achieved even less, but therein lies his strength. Noted chiefly for his indolence – Walpole wrote that 'he remained buried in Squireland ... drinking port, nursing gout, and dozing over the fire.' Very rarely bestirring himself to visit London, he was the ideal recipient of Walpole's non-political chit-chat. He would surely want to know of all the social events, the news, the gossip and scandal. He was in receipt of hundreds of letters and it is to him we are indebted for Walpole's most amusing and scintillating accounts of London life.

Another group of friends who called themselves *The Quadruple Alliance** was more significant and more intellectual, though not as privileged. They were Richard West, Thomas Ashton and Thomas Gray. West's father was a lawyer and sometime Lord Chancellor of Ireland, but Ashton and Gray were several levels of social strata below the wealthy son of the Prime Minister. This does not seem to have affected their relationship however, even though Gray's mother ran a milliner's shop in London and Ashton's father was usher in a Lancaster grammar school on a salary of £32 a year. The one great difference between them was that Gray, unlike Ashton, never wanted or expected to gain anything from such a friendship.

It is not surprising that Horace should have been so happy at Eton when we consider his family life – at that time largely ignored by his father, who was living openly with his mistress, disliked by

---

*As the son of a politician Horace would have known that there had been a more famous *Quadruple Alliance,* the pact settled in 1718 between Austria, The Netherlands, France and England, devised to prevent Spain from altering the terms of the Treaty of Utrecht.

his brothers and spoiled and over-protected by his mother. Curiously, a dysfunctional family life was one of the things the foursome had in common. West's father died when he was ten and his mother, strongly suspected of having poisoned him, immediately began an affair with his secretary. Gray's father was an eccentric – some say half-crazed – and violent man, whose brutality towards his wife led to her seeking a legal separation. It is perhaps because of this that mothers played such an important part in all their lives.

But it was their temperament, their studious, romantic and somewhat sentimental nature which drew them together into what was clearly a deeply-felt friendship. The very term *Alliance* suggests that they were, by forming a group, protecting themselves against something, and Jacob Bryant, in his memoirs printed in the *Gentleman's Magazine* in 1846, wrote that 'some ... who were severe, treated them as feminine characters, on account of their too great delicacy, and sometimes a too fastidious behaviour.' However, the *Alliance* survived and they seem to have managed to live in an Arcadian dreamland of their own, reading pastoral poetry, Dryden's plays, and the French romance novels of Mme de Scudéry. In their own Arcadia they lived under exotic names and even after leaving school, Walpole, Gray, West and Ashton continued to refer to themselves as Celadon, Oromades, Favonius and Almanzor.

They would seem to have educated themselves far beyond the classical Eton syllabus which then concentrated almost exclusively on Latin Verse, something for which Walpole did no more than was strictly necessary, telling his cousin Henry Conway, 'I remember when I was at Eton and Mr Bland had set me any extraordinary task, I used sometimes to pique myself upon not getting it, what, learn more than I was forced to learn!'

When the time came for the members of the *Alliance* to leave Eton in 1735, Horace, following the Walpole family tradition, went up to King's College, Cambridge. Ashton had already been admitted there as a scholar and Gray was dolefully in residence at Peterhouse. West was not with them; he had gone up to Christ Church, Oxford two years before and, as his letters show, was sorely missing his friends.

For the sons of gentry, university was not at that time somewhere they went to be educated and awarded a degree; it was simply somewhere they went to pass a few more years, dining and drinking, cock-fighting and badger-baiting etc (often a good deal of etc) after leaving school and before they went off on the Grand Tour. They didn't need a qualification, as they never intended to 'do' anything, except possibly enter parliament, and what qualifications did anyone ever need for that?

Walpole spent four years at Cambridge and although his attendance was, to say the least, irregular, he took his studies more seriously than most of those of his social class. From his *Short Notes of My Life* we learn that he attended lectures in civil law, philosophy, and Italian, but his true interests were not catered for. As he put it to Montagu, 'We have not the least poetry stirring here ... I have been so used to the delicate food of Parnassus that I can never condescend to apply to the grosser studies of Alma Mater ... I am not against cultivating these studies as they are certainly useful, but then they neglect all polite literature, all knowledge of this world.'

He did try to acquire some *useful* knowledge. He undertook a course in mathematics with the distinguished and blind professor Saunderson, but after two weeks the kindly professor told him it was a cheat to take his money. 'Believe me,' he said, 'you can never learn these things, you have no capacity for them.' The Strawberry Hill account books are said to show just how right he was.

During his early days at Cambridge Horace showed evidence of some religious zeal, visiting the jail along with Ashton to pray and read the Bible with the prisoners, but this did not last long and all trace of enthusiasm was eradicated when he encountered Dr Conyers Middleton, a fellow of Trinity and the University librarian. There seems little doubt that hopes of preferment attracted him to the Prime Minister's son, but unlike Ashton, he was quite refreshingly open about it, writing to ask him 'to inform Sir Robert ... that he would be proud to receive ... some mark of public favour proper to his character and profession.' In fact he received none; nevertheless they remained on the friendliest of terms. ' ... my esteem for your works makes me impatient to renew a friendship which I had contracted for your person', Walpole wrote to him some years after leaving Cambridge. They had a shared interest in classical antiques and Walpole bought Middleton's entire collection in 1744.

Middleton's influence on Walpole cannot be underestimated. Although an ordained minister of the Church of England, he took a very individual line, being dubbed 'an infidel' by many of his colleagues. He was an eloquent exponent of deism, that rather cold attitude to religion which believed not in a personal god but only in a benevolent First Cause. In his book a *Free Enquiry into Miraculous Powers* he dismissed all claims not based on reason and called in doubt the 'inspiration' of the scriptures. Walpole, always a detached observer of things as they really are, found deism satisfied him for the rest of his life, explaining to Mme Deffand:

> I believe in a future life, God has created so much that is good and beautiful that we can trust him for the rest. We should not deliberately offend him. Virtue must please him, therefore be virtuous. But Nature does not admit perfection. Therefore God will not condemn what is not according to nature. That is my profession of faith. It is very brief and very simple.

One of Middleton's passions was his hatred of priests and kings and Walpole's shared belief in this is evident in his long poem of 1740, 'An Epistle to Ashton', which ends:

> Now have I try'd of kings and priests to sing
> And all the woes that from their vices spring.

Ashton was at that time tutor to the son of the Earl of Plymouth and the poem urges him to instil in his pupil a love of liberty.

In 1737, Horace's next-to-last year in Cambridge, his mother died. Gray, perhaps alone, understood how grief-stricken he must have been and wrote immediately offering his condolences, but adding that he knew, 'Nothing I can say should lighten your affliction.' He knew just what life was like at Houghton, having written to him earlier there expressing his sympathy that he found himself living 'in a Confusion of Wine & Bawdy & Hunting & Tobacco.'

Lady Walpole was buried on the Houghton estate, but it was left to Horace, the youngest son, to arrange for a memorial to her to be placed in Westminster Abbey. Sir Robert was clearly not distressed by her death. It allowed him to marry his mistress in an extravagant ceremony six months later. Three months after that she died in childbirth. Simply being at Houghton must have been painful for Horace and in the September he ended a letter to Lyttleton, 'I am now got to Cambridge out of a house which I could not bear.'

Late in the following year he left Cambridge without taking a degree and for some time he was, as Sir Edmund Gosse put it, 'a kind of waif and stray.'

His father briefly entertained the idea that he should pursue a career in law, but happily the idea was abandoned. Instead he settled that bizarre collection of sinecures on him, a settlement which enabled him to be independent and free. Free to get away from it all. Free to travel.

2

THE GRAND TOUR

THE OED CREDITS RICHARD LASSELS WITH the earliest use of the term *The Grand Tour* in his book *The Voyage of Italy* published in 1670, but this does not mean that the phrase was not in familiar use before that date, nor that young men had not previously gone travelling in Europe. Indeed, as far back as 1570 Sir Philip Sidney observed, 'A great number of us never thought in ourselves why we went, but a curious tickling humour to do as other men had done.' It is, of course, unlikely to have been a feature of life during the Civil War, nor during Cromwell's Protectorate, but the Restoration of Charles II brought about changes so rapid and so extreme that they are hard to envisage. In dress alone, what extremes of contrast there are between our image of Milton and the coronation portraits of the King, yet they were contemporaries. The flamboyant French influence became so quickly established that by 1676 it was being satirised in such characters as Sir Foppling Flutter in George Etheredge's comedy *The Man of Mode*. And by 1741 Pope expected the readers of his 'Dunciad' to be familiar with the accepted view of young men on their Tour. Guided, as he sees them, by the great Empress of Dullness:

> Led by my hand, he saunter'd Europe round.
> And gathered ev'ry Vice on Christian Ground.

The Grand Tour, it is generally accepted, was chiefly an eighteenth-century phenomenon, pursued by the sons of the rich who had been educated in the Classics and could now be financially supported for some considerable length of time while they went off to see where such things had all begun. It was looked upon as a way of completing their education, but also as a means, it was to be hoped, of them acquiring some degree of sophistication, and, more than likely, for keeping them out of sight during that awkward period between leaving university and being married, when they might be getting into conspicuous trouble at home.

In 1739 when Horace Walpole embarked on his Tour, it was then not quite the ritualised procession it was to become. Ten years later and Tomas Nugent had published his travel guide *The Grand Tour* in which he asserted that travel would form the complete gentleman. But apart from visiting friends in Paris, Horace seems to have had no clear idea of what he was going to do when he first set out. As his travelling companion Thomas Gray put it in an early letter from Paris to their fellow Etonian, Thomas Ashton, 'We are exceedingly unsettled and irresolute, don't know our own minds for two moments together. In short, I think the greatest evil that could have happened to us is our liberty, for we are not at all capable to determine our own actions.'

We have to remember how young they were and how unused to fending for themselves. Indeed it had been his father's idea in the first place that Horace should go abroad, possibly to get him out of the way at the time of his mother's death and Sir Robert's own *o'erhasty marriage* to his mistress Maria Skerrett. And it was he who, six months into the Tour, was advising his son not to return home, but to go on to Italy. Later 'Grand Tourists' would not have needed any such advice; it was the whole object of the enterprise.

An unusual feature of Horace's travel was that he had not been provided with the customary 'bear-leader', the term given to the chaperone, usually an elderly, respected clergyman, who would accompany young men with the object of guarding their morals and trying to keep them out of trouble. Horace Walpole had no such encumbrance, but he did not travel alone. He took with him Thomas Gray, his close friend from Eton.

His choice of Gray as a travelling companion has often occasioned some surprise. True they were very different in temperament, but this is not necessarily a bar to friendship and they had been friends since they were nine years old. They knew each other better than we can ever surmise. And which of his other friends might he have chosen? Richard West, as they all knew, was not in good health (he was to die in 1742) and since he had gone to Oxford they had not been in close contact. And as for Ashton, it is likely that Horace was already suspecting him of being the toady he was.

A huge social gulf existed between Walpole and Gray, but then there always had been. The difference now though was that for the entire duration of their tour Horace would be paying for everything and this must at times have been hard for Gray to swallow. He was a proud man and knew his worth, but this was putting him in his place. The warmth of Walpole's feelings for him are, however, evident from the fact that before they left England he drew up a will declaring that were he to die while he was abroad, Gray was to inherit everything of which he was possessed, a generosity which could possibly be looked upon as patronising.

It was at noon on Easter Sunday, 29 March, 1739 that Walpole and Gray set sail from Dover on the five-hour crossing to Calais. The weather was not kind. A 'pretty brisk gale', Gray called it, admitting to being 'extremely sick the whole time'. It began to snow hard from the minute they came into the harbour, but Calais made a lasting impression on them both. Gray called it 'a very pretty town', while Walpole, writing to Richard West from Florence the following January, said, 'To speak sincerely, Calais surprised me more than anything I have seen since.' But at Calais everything would have been new, different and exciting, in a word, *foreign*. Gray was certainly taking it all in. In a letter to his mother, he described the journey to Paris so vividly. 'On every hillock is a windmill, a crucifix or a Virgin Mary dressed in flowers and a sarcenet robe ... now and then indeed you meet a strolling friar, a country-man with his great muff, or a woman riding astride on a little ass, with short petticoats and a great head-dress of blue cloth.' No, it wasn't a bit like Windsor or The Strand. And neither was the food – foreign stuff. 'We dined at Montreuil, much to our heart's content, on stinking mutton cutlets, addle eggs, and ditch water.' It seems you couldn't even get a decent cup of tea.

After Calais, Paris seems to have been something of a

disappointment, but waiting to meet them there were Horace's cousins, Francis and Henry Conway. They had all been friends at Eton and Henry was to become Horace's most intimate friend and one his most frequent correspondents right up to the time of his death in 1795. Other English residents were delighted to have the son of the Prime Minister with them, but almost immediately we can sense that their differing social status was beginning to cause problems. A letter from Gray to Richard West begins, 'Mr Walpole has gone out to supper at Lord Conway's and here I remain alone, though invited too.' He was more interested in things than people and the highpoint of his letter is a description of 'a vase of entire onyx ... at least two thousand years old ... we have dreamed of it ever since.' They were taken to the opera and agreed on their verdict, though Walpole's was more acerbic, telling West, 'their music resembles gooseberry tart as much as it does harmony.' Then they were taken to Versailles, where their opinions were what many visitors have since shared. Gray called the palace 'a huge heap of littleness', with Walpole adding, ''tis a garden for a great child.'

The essential difference between the two young men is clear in their letters. On April 21st they sat down in their apartment in the Rue des Petits Augustines to write letters: Gray to Ashton, Walpole to West. There is little of interest in what Gray has to say: a brief description of Paris and Parisians, that the Conways have shown them the sights and that the French have a passion for playing cards – a passion he clearly does not share. When we turn to Walpole, he tells West that he has 'been to one of the finest burials that ever was in France.' It was of the Marshal of France, but Horace was not impressed. He describes the procession as 'a vile thing. A long procession of flambeaux and friars.' But then, and so very casually, comes the shock.

> By the by, some of these choice monks, who watched the body while it lay in state, fell asleep one night, and let the tapers catch fire of the rich velvet mantle lined with ermine and powdered with gold flower-de-luces, which melted the lead coffin, and burned off the feet of the deceased before it wakened them.

We know whom we would rather have had letters from.

But Gray explains one problem they do encounter (though even today this comes as no surprise) – that it is very difficult to have any meaningful relationship with the French unless you speak their language, and speak it well. So in June they determined to leave the capital and spend some months of intensive study in Rheims, which, they soon decided had 'a melancholy aspect', but where they did enjoy the food and the champagne. In September, accompanied by Harry Conway, they headed south towards Dijon. Travel is so easy for us today that we need to remind ourselves of the hazards and hardships that were likely to be encountered at that time and Smollett's account in his *Travels through France and Italy* written in 1766 is probably not that exceptional:

> About half way between Montefiascone and Viterbo, one of the forewheels flew off altogether with a large splinter of the axle-tree; and if one of the postilions had not by great accident been a remarkably ingenious fellow we should have been put to the greatest inconvenience as there was no town or even house within several miles. I mention this circumstance, by way of warning to other travellers that they may provide themselves with a hammer, and nails, a spare iron-pin or two, a large knife and a bladder of grease, to be used occasionally in case of such misfortune.

From Dijon, 'what it lacks in extent is made up for in beauty and cleanliness', they made for Lyons where the streets were 'narrow and nasty.' From there they made a 'little excursion' to Geneva, where Conway left them. The route they took allowed them to visit the monastery of La Grande Chartreuse, a journey through the mountains which proved to be quite beyond Walpole's powers of description: 'But the road, West, the road, winding round a prodigious mountain and surrounded by others ... we wished for a painter, wished to be poets!' But one of them was on the cusp of becoming one of our most gifted poets, and could indeed paint a colourful picture of it to his mother:

> It is six miles to the top; the road runs winding up to it, commonly not six feet broad; on one hand is the rock, with woods of pine trees hanging overhead; on the other a monstrous precipice, almost perpendicular, at the bottom of which rolls a torrent that sometimes tumbling among the fragments of stone that have fallen from on high, and sometimes precipitating itself down vast descents with a noise like thunder, which is still made greater by the echo from the mountains on each side, concurs to form one of the most solemn, the most romantic, and astonishing views I ever beheld.

So much for the commonly held belief that Gray was afraid of mountains and thought them 'horrid'.

It was when they returned to Lyons that Walpole received a letter from his father suggesting that they continued their tour into Italy. Again it is to the letters of Thomas Gray that we turn for a full account of their adventures. And adventures they had. It took them eight days to reach Turin and as they had left it to the end of October, winter had set in. When they reached the foot of Mount Cenis it was no longer possible to travel by chaise so they were bundled up in furs, strapped onto kinds of wicker chair supported on poles and carried in this way by eight men, the six miles up and six miles down. 'The men perfectly fly down with you, stepping from stone with incredible swiftness in places where none but they could go three paces without falling.'

The scenery they found spectacular, literally awe-inspiring. Gray again, 'Not a precipice, not a torrent, not a cliff, but is pregnant with religion and poetry. There are certain scenes that would awe an atheist into belief, without the help of other argument.' One event shows the sheer wildness of the place. Walpole had taken with him his fat little King Charles spaniel, ironically named Tory, and as he told Richard West:

> I had let it out of the chaise for the air, and it waddling along close to the head of the horses [when] there darted out a young wolf, seized poor dear Tory by the throat, and before we could possibly prevent it, sprang up the side of the rock and carried him off. ... It was shocking to see anything one loved run away with to so horrid a death.

Thankfully, nothing so shocking happened again to them, but it makes us realise that these young travellers must have been more resilient than we sometimes give them credit for.

The downhill path was equally fearsome; Walpole was mightily impressed by the agility of the mountaineers, carrying them at a run down frozen precipices where, as he put it, no man could possibly walk. Sadly, we find an unpleasant example of Milord's attitude to Johnny Foreigner when Gray in a letter to Richard West refers to the same people as 'Alpine monsters ... creatures ...

in all respects, below humanity.' *Autres temps, autres mœurs,* in no way excuses it.

After a brief respite in Turin, they reached Genoa, a city which delighted Gray. As he described it in a long ecstatic letter to West, 'I never beheld anything more amiable ... palaces and churches peeping over one another's heads, gardens and marble terraces full of orange and cypress trees, fountains and trellis-works covered with vines.' This was Italy. They had even arrived on a feast day and he tells him of a statue of the Virgin Mary, 'richly dressed out, with a crown of diamonds on her head.' And then in procession came the Doge 'in his robes of crimson and damask and a cap of the same', followed by the senate in all their splendour and an orchestra and two eunuchs' voices which were 'a perfect feast' to their ears. Yes, it had been an occasion worth crossing the mountains for.

From there they moved on to Florence, arriving in mid-December 1739. The winter months in Florence were a rather dull time and after a few weeks Horace was giving vent to his boredom. 'The farther I travel,' he told West, 'the less I wonder at anything; a few days reconcile me to a new spot, or an unseen custom; and men are so much the same everywhere ... the same weakness, the same passions ... drinking, whoring.' But when Carnival began he was in his element and it was a very different Horace who wrote again to West at the end of February, 'I have done nothing but slip out of my domino [a large hooded cloak with an eye-mask worn at a masquerade] into bed, and out of bed into my domino. The end of the Carnival is frantic, bacchanalian; all the morn one makes parties in masque to the shops and coffee-houses, and all the evening to operas and balls.

Then I have danced, good gods, how I have danced.' This was probably the first chance he had ever had to enjoy himself in such a way; in England at school and college he had been in all male company and his days in France seem to have been rather staid. Not so in Florence. Gray on the other hand makes no mention of Carnival in his letters to his mother. It is hard to picture him in a domino, and in a letter to Thomas Wharton he says that Florence would enable him to write 'A learned Dissertation on the true Situation of Gomorrah ... ' What he was writing was a long poem in Latin hexameters on the philosophy of Locke De *Principiis Cogitandi*. One senses trouble ahead.

It was not all frivolity though. It was in Florence that they met Horace Mann. A minor diplomat, distantly related to the Walpoles, Mann was to play a crucial part in Horace's life, and yet we know very little about him. Another *confirmed bachelor*, he seems to have been equally fastidious, but of a more retiring and warm-hearted nature. His role in Florence when they first met in December 1739 was that of chargé d'affairs to the Ducal Court of Tuscany, an appointment awarded him by Sir Robert. His duties there consisted of keeping a watchful and kindly eye on the young British tourists passing through the city, but also of keeping a very close eye on the activities of the Stuart enclave and reporting on this to the Prime Minister. In April 1740 Horace sent him a letter by special courier to advise him that one of the Pretender's sons had 'left Rome yesterday morning under the pretence of quail shooting. I hope this will be time enough for you to send to watch him at all post-houses and to take what measures you think proper of advising the government to stop him.' It was information Mann promptly passed on to Lord Newcastle in London. The uprising of 1745 was still some years away, but we can assume that nefarious schemes were already afoot.

Despite the eleven year gap in their ages, the two Horaces became close friends from the moment they met, and of the two years and more that Walpole and Gray were in Italy, they spent over twelve months as guests of Mann in his house, the Palazzo Manetti overlooking the Arno. Curiously, however, after Walpole finally left Florence in April 1741 he and Mann were never to meet again, yet their correspondence amounts to more than 800 letters, ending only with Mann's death in 1786. As Horace had put it two years earlier, 'I have been counting how many letters I have written to you since I landed in England in 1741 – they amount – astonishingly – to above 800! and we have not met in three and forty years! A correspondence of near half a century is, I suppose, not to be paralleled in the annals of the Post Office.' Horace not only wrote to him; he looked after him; ensuring his knighthood in 1755 and a baronetcy in 1768.

Mann's replies to all these letters have been described, rather harshly perhaps, by one of Walpole's editors as 'absolutely unreadable', which does make one wonder why he persisted for all those years. But Horace chose his correspondents with care. He himself being at the centre of English political and social life and Mann being far away in Florence, his letters are largely confined to an account of the most important events of the time. Meant ultimately, as is quite evident, for publication and posterity, they are therefore among the most valuable historical documents of the eighteenth century.

As we have seen, Horace thoroughly enjoyed the frivolities of the Florentine Carnival, but when the weeks of Lent came we are shown a very different side to his nature in his long poem 'An Epistle from Florence to Thomas Ashton Esq. Tutor to the Earl of Plymouth'. This tutorship was the first of other remunerative positions he would secure for Ashton.

One of the remarkable things about eighteenth-century poetry is that even the most minor of talents never seem to put a (metrical) foot wrong. This is certainly true of Horace, but sadly, also true is the fact that once mounted on their rocking-horse couplets it was hard to rein them in, and this Epistle is very long. It can only have been their close friendship which led Gray to tell West that it was, 'full of spirit and thought and a good deal of poetic fire.'

Ostensibly its aim is to encourage Ashton to instil into his young pupil a love of liberty and a hatred of tyranny and bigotry. Or, to put it another way, the Protestant virtues as opposed to the evils of the Church of Rome, views to which Walpole, though fundamentally a deist, would remain constant. Far from adopting a reasoned argument, however, it is more of a relentless and intemperate rant and any thinking evident in it he owes, as he himself admitted, to his Cambridge tutor, Conyers Middleton.

Its central idea is asserted almost immediately.

> The greatest curses any age has known
> Have issued from the temple and the throne.
> Extent of ill from Kings at first begins
> But priests must aid and consecrate their sins.

To demonstrate the truth of this we are treated to a gallop

through a gallery of English monarchs from John to George. There are some good moments, such as the description of Henry VIII:

> Big in unwieldly majesty and pride
> And smear'd with queens and martyrs blood he dy'd.

Charles I is partially forgiven, as much of the blame can be attributed to his Catholic wife:

> To lustful Henrietta's Romish shade
> Let all his acts of lawless pow'r be laid.

Anti-Jacobin feelings were very much in the air at that time and no excuses could be made for Charles II:

> The care of nations left to whores or chance
> Plund'rer of Britain, pensioner of France,
> Free to Buffoons, to ministers deny'd,
> He liv'd an atheist, and a bigot dy'd.

The poem ends with a curt nod in the direction of George II.

For all this anti-papist zeal, there was something about the splendour of Roman Catholic rituals which held an attraction for both Gray and Walpole and when the death of Pope Clement XII was announced in February 1740 they could not wait to get to Rome to witness the Conclave of cardinals, but the proceedings dragged on and by the end of June a decision still had not been reached. Horace explained to his cousin Henry Conway, 'I did intend to stay for a new popedom, but the old eminences are cross and obstinate and will not choose one; the Holy Ghost knows when.'

Rome was not to Horace's liking and in a city where Jacobite sentiments were so strong, he, as the Prime Minister's son, would not have been made to feel especially welcome; raising, and with good reason, their political suspicions. With the approach of hot weather and the real fear of malaria, he decided to return to Florence. They went by way of Herculaneum which fascinated Gray, and for once Horace shared his enthusiasm. This was not sight-seeing, this was the epitome of antiquarianism. The site had only been found by chance a year and a half previously and he wrote to West, 'This underground city is perhaps one of the noblest curiosities that has ever been discovered ... they have found among other things some fine statues, some human bones, some rice, medals, and a few paintings extremely fine.' This must have been so exciting, but at other times we can see him getting tired of monuments and ruins and in a letter to Ashton he seems to have been referring to Gray's journal when he writes:

> By a considerable volume of charts and pyramids, which I saw at Florence, I thought it threatened a publication. His travels here have really improved him. I wish they may do the same for anyone else.

And Ashton, who was probably envious of Gray having been chosen as Horace's travelling companion, might, unwisely, have been led to feel that such remarks, together with the Epistle, meant that he now rated the higher in Walpole's estimation. If so, it was a feeling soon to have serious consequences.

One can sense the beginnings of a rift. Walpole and Gray had been together every day for two years, so it is remarkable that it had not come about sooner. Gray had not wanted to leave Rome. Now Walpole, who had grown tired of inscriptions and columns, did not want to leave Florence, especially as so many new and interesting people were arriving. Among them was a pair of travellers who could have hardly seemed more ill-matched. Francis Whithed was a wealthy, but morose, partly deaf and sickly young man of twenty-three, who was travelling, not with the usual *bearward*, but with his impoverished forty-year old cousin, John Chute, a man so theatrically high camp as to have been seen frequently with a quizzing glass in one hand and a fan in the other. Horace used to refer to them as *The Chutheds.* As a group, Mann, Gray, Horace and The Chutheds must have turned a few heads when they were seen out together, but Chute was to become a close friend and to play a particularly important role in the life at Strawberry Hill.

But the time had come for them to return home. Frederick II of Prussia had invaded Silesia; a European war looked threatening and Sir Robert, who was now fast losing power, urged his son to put an end to his travels. Family loyalty would always exercise a strong pull on Horace and so, reluctantly and perhaps a little out of humour, he and Gray packed up their belongings and set off. One of the first stops on their way was Reggio, and it was in that 'dirty little place', as Walpole called it, that something happened to bring about their separation.

Various themes have been proposed to explain this breach; one being that Horace suspected that Gray was being critical of him in his correspondence with West and Ashton, and so opened one of his letters. Such an idea is quite out of the question. Horace Walpole was a gentleman and would never for one moment have even contemplated opening another gentleman's letters. And even if he had done so, would he have confessed to it? It is feasible that

Gray may have been indiscreet in some of his letters. For instance, in a letter of 21st April, after telling West of the ways he had changed in the years he had been abroad, particularly his failings, he added, 'On the good side you may add a sensibility for what others feel, and indulgence for their faults or weaknesses.' Could this not be looked on as an implied criticism of Walpole's lack of such sensibility? Added to which he also wrote, 'I must own I have the vanity of desiring to be esteemed by somebody.' There is a sense of injured pride there; he had been the dependant for a long time and if Ashton had picked up on any such adverse remarks, he would have been very quick to let Horace know.

A letter of some kind does seem to have been an issue, as Mann, trying to clear the air, told Horace that, 'except writing that letter he was not so much to blame as on the sight of it you might imagine.' Mann did his best to bring about a reconciliation, writing to him again towards the end of May, 'I can only say that you have it in you to do a most generous action, to forget and forgive. I would ask it on my knees if I was with you.' But it was no use; the pride of two very proud young men had been hurt. We cannot hope to know exactly what happened, but all of us know that in any close relationship the tiniest thing can escalate out of all proportion. What we also have to keep in mind is that these were two young men who had 'had the time of their lives.' They had seen some of the finest buildings in Europe: Notre Dame and St Peters. In crossing the Alps they had encountered hardship, danger, excitement and the most sublime beauty. They had visited the most vibrant cities: Paris, Naples, Venice, Florence and Rome. They had been welcomed and entertained wherever they went. But now it was all coming to an end and that was not something either was looking forward to. Horace wrote to Conway, 'I know the causes that drove me out of England, and I don't know that they are remedied.' Gray was aware that he would never again live as he had for the past two years. The glamour was over and the time was ripe for the slightest tiff to turn into a quarrel. As Norton Nicholls was to write in his *Reminiscences,* 'I agree with Mr Mason who once said to me that it was more surprising that two persons of characters so opposite to each other should ever have agreed than that they should have finally separated'.

When Gray left Reggio, Chute and Whithed went with him, which suggests that he was seen by them at least as the injured party. Not long after, and perhaps brought on by stress, Horace contracted quinsy and was seriously ill. Fortunately, Joseph Spence, the Professor of Poetry at Oxford, chanced to be in Reggio. They had met the year before in Florence and Spence took charge of the situation. Without him there is every chance that Horace, whom Spence later described as 'one of the best natured and most sensible young gentlemen that England affords', might well have died.

On his return to England in September 1741 Horace had soon established a much warmer relationship with his father and had taken his seat in the Commons as member for Callington in Cornwall, having been elected to it in his absence the previous May. It was a constituency which he represented for over a decade but which he never once visited, though he did contemplate bestowing on one of his pet dogs the title of Viscount Callington.

Gray's return was less eventful. Staying again at La Grande Chartreuse he wrote a Latin poem in their guest book. Its closing lines read, in translation, 'Father, that I may pass the untroubled hours of old age in some secluded corner and bear me off unharmed from the tumult of the crowds and the cares of men.'

The secluded corner he chose was his old Cambridge college, Peterhouse, but sadly he was not unharmed there. His prudish manners attracted attention and he was mimicked, harassed and tormented by that exuberant poet Christopher Smart and his cronies. Apparently, he used to walk with little mincing steps, with his head in the air and one hand behind his back holding up his gown. 'Gray walks as though he had fouled his small clothes and looks as though he smelt it,' was Smart's cruel and memorable observation.

Happily, in 1746 there was a reconciliation between Horace and Gray and although somewhat uneasy at first, their old friendship was slowly resumed.

Gray died in 1771, aged 55, and two years later his friend William Mason wrote to Horace asking him if he could provide him with a brief account of their estrangement for a biography. Horace did, but more tellingly he also wrote privately and at length.

> ... the fault was mine. I was too young, too fond of my own diversions, nay, I do not doubt too much intoxicated, by indulgence, vanity and the insolence of my situation as a Prime Minister's son, not to have been inattentive and insensible to the feelings of one I thought below me ... I treated him insolently; he loved me and I did not think he did. I reproached him with the difference between us ... I often disregarded his wishes of seeing places, which I would not quit my amusement to visit, though I offered to send him to them without me. Forgive me if I say that his temper was not conciliating, at the same time that I will confess to you that he acted a more friendly part, had I had the sense to

take advantage of it. He freely told me of my faults. I declared that I did not want to hear them, nor would correct them. You will not wonder that the dignity of his spirit, and the obstinate carelessness of mine, the breach must have grown wider, till we became incompatible.

We notice that he fails to give specific details of what caused the quarrel, but in laying so much of the blame on himself, it is the letter of a gentleman. There were, however, faults on both sides. As Horace said, Gray's 'temper was not conciliating'. He could be touchy and intolerant and Johnson, though he had little time for him, may have nevertheless put his finger on it when he wrote in his *Life of Gray*:

> If we look, however, without prejudice on the world we shall find that men, whose consciousness of their own merit sets them above the compliances of servility, are apt enough in their association with superiors to watch their own dignity with troublesome and punctilious jealousy, and in the fervour of independence to exact that attention which they refuse to pay.

3
HOUGHTON HALL

THERE IS LITTLE DOUBT THAT THE quarrel at Reggio was of singular importance in the lives of both Gray and Walpole, but it does tend to overshadow other aspects of their Grand Tour, in particular that these were the years which laid the groundwork for Walpole becoming one of the most distinguished antiquaries of his day – indeed to his being proclaimed the *Prime Minister of Taste.* However, when we read the letters he wrote home to friends and relatives, the 'facts' which we glean look to be as contradictory and complex as we have begun to expect.

When, fifty years later, he was looking back on his time in Florence, he told his friend Mary Berry how he had enjoyed, 'the delicious nights on the Ponte de Trinita at Florence, in a linen nightgown and a straw hat with *improvisatori,* music and the coffee-houses open with ices.' While there, he told Henry Conway that it was all 'operas, concerts, and balls, mornings and evenings.' Yet sometimes he would have people believe how bored he was becoming by it all, telling Richard West, 'I am grown so used to being surprised that I don't perceive any flutter in myself when I meet with any novelties; curiosity and astonishment wear off.' A certain blasé air was essential if one didn't want to be taken for a tourist. Yet only a week later he is writing, again to Conway, 'How I like the inanimate part of Rome you will soon perceive at my arrival in England; I am far gone in medals, lamps, idols, prints etc. and all the small commodities to the purchase of which I can attain; I would buy the Coliseum if I could.' This is endorsed in a letter to Horace Mann shortly after he did arrive home. 'I write to you up to the head and ears in dirt, straw and unpacking. I have been opening all my cases from the Custom House all morning.'

These contrasting sides to his nature are clearly illustrated in the portrait painted of him by Reynolds in 1757. His lace-cuffed hand is resting gently against his cheek. Nonchalant and graceful, he is in pensive mood. Looking directly at us, there is in his expression something almost supercilious, something ever so slightly bored. All in all, it is the pose of a gentleman, but on the table beside him, curled casually as though it were there by mere chance, is a print portraying the splendid and costly antique bronze eagle which he had bought in Florence after complex and protracted negotiations and which was one day destined to occupy pride of place in the Long Gallery of Strawberry Hill.

The portrait is the epitome of *Sprezzatura*. He wants to be *seen* to possess that costly and beautiful bronze, but to have included it in the picture would have looked ostentatious and ungentlemanly. Instead, it is meant to look as though the print simply happens to be there; it is only just evident and one has to look for it. He does not want to be seen as a collector. In those cricketing terms of long ago, he was a *Gentleman* who did not want to be taken for a *Player*. But when in contact with another *Player*, he drops the guise. Conyers Middleton was a respected antiquary of note and so Horace is quite open with him about what he has acquired – open enough even to boast a little. His list includes a bust of Vespasian in 'the finest black marble'. Then there are several other smaller busts, some votive offerings and lamps and 'a small cestrum which is very uncommon', plus 'a Ceres with silver eyes and a cow in her lap' and 'some Etruscan urns'. This is hardly a run-of-the-mill collection and as Middleton says in his reply, 'I was not mistaken in my notion of your manner of spending your time as well as money in Italy and congratulate you on the importing of these curious pieces.'

All these 'curious pieces' were carefully displayed in his house in Arlington Street, but it was not long after he was settled there that Sir Robert lost a crucial vote in the Commons and resigned. His move from Downing Street to Houghton Hall meant that a new home had to be found for the hundreds of pictures he had acquired and Horace undertook not only the design of the new gallery, but where and how each painting was to be hung.

***

Horace had not been looking forward to coming back to England, and even six years later, writing to Mann, he is still wishing he was back in Florence – 'I never was happy but there; have millions of times repented returning to England where I never was happy, nor expect to be.' And again, 'I can truly say that I never was happy but at Florence.' And yet, though he often voiced his intention of going back, he never did. And it was not that he was averse to travel; he visited Paris at least five times. Had he been the dilettante he has so often been accused of being, it is easy to imagine him frittering his time away in a pretty palazzo, charming the contessas and discussing objects of vertu with wealthy collectors. But Walpole was too sensible not to see the futility of such an existence. He would have realised that when he was no longer the son of the Prime Minister, but simply a young man, an ex-pat, without title or wealth, his social standing would have been greatly reduced, and that was something he would not have relished. But there were other, more important factors too: loyalty and duty – to his family and his country. One should never underestimate the significance he put on being a member of parliament, which he was for 27 years. There he witnessed first hand and played his own part in the most important events of the time. London, not Florence, was where history was being made, where greatness was, and where it could be recorded. These great events he recounted in his letters to Horace Mann, letters which can be seen as a rehearsal for his later political memoirs – letters which he had from the very start looked upon as being meant for posterity, and which have ever since been a primary source for historians of his time.

Loyalty to his family had an equal pull. He cared for his nephews and nieces, helping to secure them advantageous marriages. He even cared for his father's illegitimate daughter and to his great credit he cared for Sir Robert in his failing years, though they had never been very close before he left to go on his travels. Probably – time having passed – he was now able to feel some sympathy for him that in 1738, nine months after his marriage to his mistress Maria Skerrett, she had died in childbirth.

Sir Robert's fall from power had not been gracious; such events rarely are. He had still held a safe majority in the Commons when Horace came back to England, but ominously things were beginning to go wrong. Throughout most of his time in power his fixed policy had been to keep the country out of costly European conflicts, so ensuring low taxation and prosperity, but a trade dispute with Spain in 1739 was used by some of his opponents as a lever to force him into a war which he found difficult to handle. Poor election results followed in 1741 and members of his own party were now opposing him. The loss of a confidence vote in February 1742 finally brought about his resignation. In the wild, when an alpha male loses his place as head of the pack, young bloods soon move in on him and a cabal in parliament lost no time in setting up a committee to investigate every aspect of his administration with a view to impeachment and the threat of The Tower. However, no evidence of any wrong doing could be found and enthusiasm for it eventually faded.

Horace, rising to speak for the first time in the Commons, had defended his father and sent a copy of the speech to Mann, ' ... it is the strongest proof of innocence, that for twenty years together, no crime could be solemnly alleged against him; and since his dismission, he has seen a majority rise up to defend his character in that very House of Commons in which a majority had overturned his power.' Sir Robert had not however lost the support and favour of the King who immediately created him Earl of Orford, Viscount Walpole and Baron Walpole of Houghton. Ten Downing Street had been a personal gift from the King, and he was therefore obliged to leave there and take up residence in Houghton. It was only after that that Downing Street become the official residence of the Prime Minister.

Living in Houghton was not a prospect which filled Horace's heart with great joy. After the sophistication of Florentine society, how would he cope with the beer-swilling, fox-hunting, rowdy gentry of Norfolk? The picture of life there he describes in a letter to John Chute is vividly brutal.

> Only imagine that I see here everyday men, who are mountains of roast beef, and only seem just roughly hewn out into the outlines of human form ... I shudder when I see them brandish their knives in act to carve, and look on them as savages that devour one another. I should not stare more than I do if yonder Alderman at the lower end of the table was to stick his fork into his neighbour's jolly cheek, and carve a slice of brown and fat ... Oh! my dear Sir, don't you find that nine parts in ten of the world are of no use but to make you wish you were with that tenth part?

But when Sir Robert's health began to fail and his fair-weather political friends began to desert him, life quietened down and Houghton was again as he had first seen it while on a visit from Cambridge in 1736, the year after the building work was completed. He had then spent some time there almost by himself and, writing to Charles Lyttleton, declared, 'Houghton is woody and full of delightful prospects ... we have a charming garden, all wilderness and much adapted to my romantic inclinations.' On the same day, he assured his father, 'I should not have felt half the satisfaction, if it had not been your doing' and added somewhat presciently, 'I wish all your other actions could afford you as much ease to enjoy your success, as those at Houghton do.'

***

The Walpoles were not an aristocratic family. They traced their roots back through a long line of Norfolk yeoman farmers who, as the years passed, had acquired more land, more money, more social position and more power until they were among the leading members of that most influential eighteenth-century political group, the landed gentry. Robert had been born in 1676, entering Parliament in 1701. In 1721 he became First Lord of the Treasury – *de facto* Prime Minister, receiving a knighthood in 1726. Just before entering Parliament he had married Catherine Shorter, the daughter of a wealthy Baltic timber merchant who brought with her a dowry of £20,000. Adding to this by skilfully managing to sell his shares in the notorious South Sea Company at just the right moment, he acquired sufficient fortune to build Houghton Hall.

It was not long after building had begun in 1722 that it became clear just how vast it was going to be, and bearing in mind that this upstart MP was plain Mr Robert Walpole at that time – he didn't even have a knighthood – it is easy to understand the outrage it occasioned in certain aristocratic and Tory circles where his success was keenly resented. It was condemned as vulgar and ostentatious. Who did he think he was, and where was the money coming from? But Mr Walpole not only knew who he was, he knew quite well who he was going to be. And no, he had not had his hand in the public purse; when he died he left behind debts of £50,000. It was a debt which caused Horace some concern, as he put it to Mann, 'If he had not overdone it, he might have left such an estate to his family as might have secured the glory of the place for many years; another such debt must expose it to sale.' This was shortly after his father's death and while his fears at that time proved to be unfounded, three decades later, the gambling lunatic third earl sold off the pictures and anything else of value and it began to fall into ruin.

Houghton had taken fourteen years to complete and the result is one of the finest Palladian mansions in the country and was intended from the outset to be a demonstration of Walpole's wealth and power. It is massive and grand, but it is also dignified and almost austere; the only really eye-catching feature being the domed towers designed by its first architect James Gibbs, who was dismissed after only three years – it is suggested he was expecting to be paid. His successor was Colin Campbell, whose loathing of Gibbs was warmly reciprocated.

The 23 acres of grounds in which the house was set were equally grand. Designed by Eyre, an imitator of the more famous Charles Bridgeman, they are an early part of the movement away from the symmetrical French mode which had long been in fashion. He introduced winding paths which gave onto unexpected rustic views, and as Horace put it in his essay *On Modern Gardening* 'The garden in its turn was to be set free from its prim regularity that it might assort with the wilder country without.'

If the façade of Houghton Hall can seem austere, inside it is total opulence and chiefly the work of William Kent, a designer of genius. Kent's career is itself an astonishing story. Born in Bridlington, Yorkshire in 1685, he began work as a humble sign and coach painter, but a group of perceptive local business men recognised his latent ability and paid to send him to study painting in Italy. There he caught the attention and the patronage of Robert

Boyle, Earl of Burlington, to whom Pope was later to address his *Epistle IV* on Architecture and Gardening. Despite the social difference they became friends and on returning to England the Earl commissioned Kent to decorate the new state rooms in Kensington Palace. However, interior design was not his only skill. Horace wrote of him ' ... painter and architect and the father of modern gardening; in the first character he was below mediocrity, in the second he was the restorer of the science, but in the third an original, and the inventor of an art that realizes painting and improves nature. Mahomet imagined an Elysium, Kent created many.' Walpole is also responsible for the famous acclamation, 'He [Kent] leaped the fence, and saw that all Nature was a garden.'

But while Houghton's gardens were the work of Bridgeman, the interior is totally Kent's, from the overall design down to the smallest item of furniture and tiniest detail of decoration. The imposing entrance salon is a 40ft cube made almost entirely of marble with an eye-catching bust of Sir Robert wearing a toga – the very image of a Roman senator, thus leaving his visitors in no doubt as to the standing of their host. The grand staircase and much of the rest of the woodwork in the house is of the most costly mahogany, especially shipped from Cuba and the West Indies, particularly noticeable being the intricate carvings around the chimney pieces the work of Grinling Gibbons. The ceilings are everywhere sumptuously painted with classical and mythological figures: Venus appropriately in the great green bedchamber, Bacchus in the dining room; the walls lined with crimson and green silk velvet. No expense was spared and none declared, as Sir Robert deliberately burned the invoices so that no one would ever know how much he had actually spent.

Of all the splendid rooms the most important was the gallery which housed Sir Robert's collection of pictures, probably the finest in the country, containing works by Da Vinci, Michelangelo, Rubens, Vandyke, Rembrandt, Holbein, Poussin, Velazquez and so many others. When the Downing Street collection had to be added to all these, it was Horace who had the gallery redesigned to accommodate them, basing the ceiling on Serlio's in the library of St Mark's in Venice and a frieze on that of the Sybil's Temple in Tivoli. But he did not content himself simply with the hanging of these new acquisitions, he set himself the task of cataloguing the entire collection.

Aedes Walpolianae, (the House of the Walpoles) as it was called, was published privately in 1747 in an edition of only 100 copies, with a larger second edition being published by Dodsley in 1752 and a third in 1767. It was then reprinted in *The Norfolk Tour* in 1795, two years before Horace's death. Simply as a catalogue it would have been of inestimable value to anyone visiting the Hall in the days when the pictures were still there hanging on its walls. It takes us on a tour, room by room, starting at the Small Break-fast Room, until eighteen rooms later, having passed through such delights as The Hunting Hall, the Coffee-Room, and the Blue Damask Bed-Chamber, we finally come to The Gallery itself.

Each room is described in brief but precise detail. To give one example: 'The Velvet Bed-chamber is twenty-one feet and a half, by twenty-two feet and a half; the bed is of green velvet, richly embroidered and laced with gold; the ornaments designed by

Kent; the hangings are tapestry, representing the loves of Venus and Adonis, after Albano.' It is awesome to consider the hours of repetitious measuring and recording which must have gone into the making of such a catalogue. Each and every picture in each and every room is identified and described, frequently with added snippets of information.

It was a catalogue, but that is not all it was. It was intended also to be a celebration of his father's achievement and as we can see from the opening dedication it was a further statement in defence of his father's honour – 'Your power and your great wealth speak themselves in the grandeur of the whole building ... And give me leave to say, Sir, your enjoying the latter after losing the former is the brightest proof how honest were the foundations of both.' A direct refutation of the attempted impeachment and such an elegant sentence.

The work's title, *Aedes Walpolianae* is itself an indication that it is meant to glorify the family name and to establish its aristocratic status, even though Sir Robert had not been raised to the peerage until 1742, five years before. The Dedication manages to conclude with a reference to their ancestry – 'Could those virtuous men your father and grandfather arise from yonder church, how would they be amazed to see this noble edifice and spacious plantations, where once stood their plain and homely dwelling! How would they be satisfied to find only the mansion house, not the morals of the family altered!' Perhaps even more amazement might have struck his maternal grandfather who had been a timber merchant.

It is an attitude which we find reflected later in his account of several of the pictures where a noble provenance seems to be of more importance than its aesthetic value. Of a Vandyke 'Holy Family' he is at pains to point out that it once belonged to Charles I, and of a portrait of George I by Kneller he says that 'It is the only portrait for which he ever sat in England.'

His Introduction begins with a claim which it would be hard to refute, 'There are not a great many collections left in Italy more worth seeing than this at Houghton; in the preservation of the pictures it certainly excels most of them.' He goes on to claim that, 'there are enough here for any man who studies painting to form very true ideas of most of the chief heads.' This seems to give him leave to lay down his own ideas, and seemingly to exclude himself when he says of art criticism that there is 'no science whose productions are so capricious and uncertain of value.' His biographer R.W. Ketton-Cremer, usually so sympathetic, could not have put it better when he said that 'The art criticism of any period inevitably causes pain and bewilderment to future generations, and Horace Walpole's is no exception.' Horace's comments on individual paintings hardly count as criticism as there is no real attempt at evaluation. He is content with words such as 'pleasing', 'agreeable', 'exceedingly fine'. It is when he gives his opinion on schools and individuals that he gives pain.

With all the over-confidence of a young man in his late twenties he was only too eager to follow his family's motto *Fari quae sentiat* – 'Say what you feel'. Michelangelo 'was much too fond of muscles as Rubens was afterwards of flesh.' The Florentine School is dismissed in a sentence, 'Their drawing was hard and their colouring gaudy and gothic.' And similarly, the Dutch, 'those drudging Mimics of Nature's most uncomely coarseness.' Even his praise can be just as shocking, 'Spagnolet, one of the few good painters produced by Spain.' His final paragraph is summed up by Ketton-Cremer, and rightly so, as 'resounding nonsense'.

And yet there are moments when young Horace shows evidence of the keen eye he had and of his prodigious memory, as when he recognises two pictures of the Virgin by Luca Giordano as 'finished designs for two large pictures which he painted for the fine church of Madonna della Salute at Venice.'

Of little practical value any longer as the pictures are no longer there, the work is nevertheless worth dipping into for its Walponian asides and anecdotes. Of a portrait of Pope Innocent X by Velázquez we are told that 'This pope was reckoned the ugliest man of his time.' Of an 'Adoration of the Magi' by Bruegel, 'There are a multitude of little figures, all finished with the greatest Dutch exactness; the ideas too are a little Dutch for the Ethiopian King is dressed in a surplice with boots and spurs.' And of a hunting piece depicting his father, 'He is upon a white horse called The Chevalier, which was taken in Scotland in the year 1715, and was the only horse the Pretender mounted there.'

The catalogue concludes with *A Sermon on Painting*, which although preached before Lord Orford by his chaplain, had been written by Horace himself in 1742. He had taken as his text Psalm 115:5 'They have mouths but they speak not; Eyes they have but they see not.' From the outset it is an attack on the Roman Catholic church. 'I must remark to you that the words in the text, though spoken of images, which were more particularly the gods of the ancients, are equally referable to the pictures of the Romish Church and it is to them I shall chiefly confine this discourse.' There is in fact very little in the sermon about painting and considering how many *Romish* pictures featured in the Houghton collection, much of what follows does tend to seem somewhat ironic. There is a distinct shortage of logic in his argument – 'Where is the good priest?' he asks. If there were any, ' ... then were painting united with devotion and ransomed from idolatry.' Unfortunately there is no such thing as a good Romish priest, they worship idols, the creation rather than the Creator. English paintings present no such problem of course. Houghton had Kneller's portraits of William III and George I, which show 'with what fire, what love of mankind, William flew to save religion and liberty! It expresses how honest, how benign the line of HANOVER', and this from a young man who had been attacking monarchy only a few years earlier in his 'Letter to Ashton'. With all this expressed in such pompous, high-flown rhetoric, one might almost mistake it for a parody, but it is perhaps best seen as the effort of a young man to please and impress his father. Art and their love of collecting was what they had in common and which must have brought them closer together.

In all likelihood, both father and son knew that he had little time left and Lord Orford died at his house in Arlington Street on 18th March 1745, at the age of sixty-nine. By the end of 1744 he had been diagnosed as suffering from bladder stones, and despite Horace's protests he was dosed with a virulent concoction of alkaline salts known as Lixivium Lithontripticum. It could be said to have 'worked' as Sir Robert passed one large stone and fifteen fragments, but the pain, as one can well imagine, was excruciating and Horace recorded his father declaring, 'Dear Horace, this Lixivium has blown me up. It has tore me to pieces ... That it be short is all I desire. Give me more opium; knock me down ... Dear Horace, if one must die, 'tis hard to die in pain.'

This would seem to be contradicted by Horace's account of his father's death in a letter to Horace Mann of April 1745: 'His fortune attended him to the last; for he died of the most painful of all distempers with little or no pain.' Perhaps what he means, and it is to be hoped, that in his final moments the opium had indeed knocked him down.

Sadly, if Sir Robert's downfall was rapid, so was that of Houghton Hall. When his eldest son, also called Robert, became the Second Earl of Orford, he found that he had inherited debts amounting to £50,000. Nothing he did improved the situation and when he died in 1751, his son George became the Third Earl and lived, one might say regrettably, for another 40 years. A wastrel and a gambler, he even gambled away the Hall's outer staircase to someone on the lookout for some fine stonework. He was also given to fits of violent insanity, needing to be confined on several occasions. When Horace was obliged to go there in 1773 to try and sort out the financial chaos he was devastated by what he found, telling Lady Ossory:

> Judge then what I felt at finding it half a ruin, though the pictures, the glorious pictures, and furniture are in general admirably well preserved. All the rest is destruction and desolation! The two great staircases exposed to all weathers; every room in the wings rotting with wet; the ceiling of the gallery in danger; the chancel of the church unroofed; the garden a common; the park half covered with nettles and weeds; the walls and pales in ruin.

But things were to get far worse. In 1779, needing cash, George sold the entire collection of paintings to Catherine the Great of Russia for £45,000 where it formed the core of what is now The Hermitage Collection.

Horace's despair at that event is evident in a letter to Mann of December 1778

> What I have long apprehended is on the point of conclusion, the sale of the pictures at Houghton. The mad master has sent his final demand of forty-five thousand for them to the Empress of Russia, at the same time as he has been what he calls improving the outside of the house; *basta!* Thus end all my visions about Houghton, which I will never see, though I must go thither at last; nor, if I can help it, think of more.

On the death of George in 1791 Horace became the Fourth Earl, an honour which gave him no pleasure whatsoever, as he told Lady Ossory

> I am not vain in being the poorest earl in England; nor delighted to have outlived all my family, its estate and Houghton, which while it was *complete* would have given me so much pleasure; now it will only be a mortifying ruin, which I will never see.

And he never did go back, until he was buried there alongside his mother and father and his brothers.

In his last years, while being swamped by tedious and time-consuming negotiations with lawyers, agents and tenants, he did manage to secure the inheritance for the grandson of his sister Lady Mary, who had married the Third Earl of Cholmondeley, but they preferred their house in Cheshire and Houghton remained an ugly sleeping beauty through most of the nineteenth century, luckily being spared Victorian *improvements*. Then in 1918, Sibyl Sassoon, the American Rothschild heiress, who had married the Fifth Marquis Cholmondeley fell in love with the house and spent a vast amount of time and money in restoring it to something approaching its former glory, a state which the present Cholmondeleys, who regard it as their home, are happily intent on preserving.

4

STRAWBERRY HILL

WHEN HORACE ARRIVED BACK IN LONDON in September 1741 at the end of his two-year Grand Tour, he lost no time in picking up the social life he had grown used to while abroad; his letters are full of accounts of visits to the theatre, of balls and masquerades. To Mann he wrote a lively description of the new pleasure gardens of Ranelagh, which had cost £16.000 to build and where 'everybody that loves eating, drinking, staring or crowding is admitted for twelve-pence.' But by 1744 it seems that non-stop festivity and frivolity had begun to lose some of its attraction and he is now telling Mann, 'If I had a house of my own in the country, and could live there now and then alone, or frequently changing my company, I am persuaded I would like it, or at least I fancy I would.' Solitude always had its attractions for him; he preferred to travel alone, and this must have been something he was seriously contemplating, not a mere daydream, as it cannot simply have been chance that led him to that little cottage in Twickenham, on which he first took out a lease in 1747.

Twickenham was then a small and delightful town in its own right, surrounded by fields and pleasantly situated on a long curve of the River Thames. Quiet, but not excessively rural. Close enough to London, it could be reached comfortably by coach in under two hours, hence it had become a place much favoured by the wealthy and Horace counted himself fortunate in securing one of the last sites still available for development. Nearby were Hampton Court, Kew, and the grandeur of Lord Burlington's Garden at Chiswick. Fashionable as it was, it had also attracted writers: Fielding, Thomson, William Collins, Lady Mary Wortley Montagu, and of course, most famously, Alexander Pope.

It was indeed the location which had first attracted Horace, not the house. Describing it to Mann in 1747 he wrote:

> The house is so small I can send it to you in a letter to look at; the prospect is as delightful as possible; commanding the river, the town and Richmond Park, and being situated on a hill descends to the Thames through two or three little meadows, where I have some Turkish sheep and two cows, all studied in their colours for becoming the view. This little rural bijou was Mrs Chenevix's, the toy woman.

Mrs Chenevix was the owner of the house and from whom he first leased it, but her shop was not a toyshop in our understanding of the word. It did not sell toys for children, but fashionable and expensive trinkets for the very wealthy, and Horace liked to pretend, as he did in a letter to Henry Conway a few days later, that his new house was simply one of the little baubles he had seen in her shop window. Small it certainly was. Lady Townsend, when she first saw it, exclaimed, 'Lord God! Jesus! What a house,' as she climbed the stairs, 'It is just such a house as a parson's, where the children lie at the foot of the bed.' But it grew and grew, extension after extension, until forty years later it had 22 rooms and the original garden which had been no more than five acres then covered 46.

The house had originally been built by Lord Bradford's coachman and was known locally as *Chopped Straw Hall*, as he was said to have swindled his master by feeding his horses on straw and then used the profit from the hay to build it. Fortunately, Horace discovered among the deeds that it had earlier been called *Strawberry Hill,* though 'Hill' seems something of a misnomer as the highest point in the garden is hardly more than 30 feet above the level of the river. But *Strawberry Hill* it became and was Horace's home for the rest of his life.

It is hard now to form any clear picture of exactly what it was that he had bought. It must have been very odd-looking: L-shaped and partly two and partly three-storeyed. Compared with Houghton and Walterton it was certainly small – the desire to be different might itself have been part of its attraction – but he exaggerates for the fun of it. Rather unprepossessing it might have been, but it was not some pokey little thing. Previous tenants had been a duke and a bishop, so it was unquestionably more than adequate. Indeed Horace saw no immediate need, and was certainly in no hurry to make any significant improvements. Two years after moving in, he was still only thinking about it. 'Did I tell you,' he writes to George Montagu in September 1749, 'that I have found a text in Deuteronomy to authorize my future battlements? "When thou buildest a new house, then shalt thou make a battlement for thy roof, that thou bring not blood upon thy house, if any man shall fall from thence ... " It is a light-hearted attitude which continues throughout the forty or so years it took him to transform this unremarkable little house into a Gothic extravaganza.

Gothic. It is a word which sends out so many mixed messages, especially now when it can be applied equally to music, fashion, hair-styles and make-up. Even when referring to buildings, it was never meant to suggest that it was a style of architecture invented by the actual Goths. Primarily it had been used as a term of abuse. At the close of the so-called Middle Ages, the Renaissance favoured a return to what it saw as the classical principles of symmetry, balance and simplicity as exemplified by the Acropolis and the Pantheon. In his *Lives of the Artists,* written in 1550, Giorgio Vasari roundly attacked a movement which he saw as 'monstrous and barbaric', a style 'wholly ignorant of any accepted ideas of sense and order.' It was, he said, 'invented by the Goths ... it was they who made the vault with pointed arches and filled the whole of Italy with their accursed buildings.' Gothic was seen then as not only barbaric but Northern. But that, John Ruskin insisted, was its strength. In his seminal essay of 1852, *The Nature of Gothic* he asserted, 'It is true, it is greatly and deeply true that the architecture of the North is rude and wild; but it is not true that, for this reason, we are to condemn or despise it. Far otherwise, I believe it is in this very character that it deserves our profoundest reverence.'

Viewed simply in terms of church architecture, Gothic can be seen as the dominant – albeit varied – form from the reign of William the Conqueror right up to that of Henry VIII. Not of course that they knew that what they were building was called Gothic, any more than that they knew they were living in *The*

Middle Ages. The full implications of the word only became evident when the style first began to fall from favour and then came under attack.

Extensive building in stone was one of the happier consequences of the genocidal Norman invasion. Their earliest churches had tended to be somewhat square, squat and dumpy, but later the decorative element which was the hallmark of the Gothic became paramount, with gargoyles, corbels, intricate fan vaulting and foliage. The innovations of the pointed arch and the flying buttress meant that far more weight could be supported and as a result walls grew higher, spires soared into the sky and windows became larger. Before long there was stained glass in those windows and then came the glory of the great rose windows which filled cathedrals not only with light but colour.

Gothic architecture's temporary fall from grace was both a cultural and a religious phenomenon. The Reformation's introduction of the new depended upon the wholesale destruction of what was old and crucially the 'dissolution' of the country's great abbeys, Fountains, Glastonbury and Furness. Cultural vandalism on a par with our woke activists occurred on an appalling scale: the smashing of statues, altars, stained-glass windows. Before long, everywhere in the country there were crumbling ruins, overgrown with ivy and haunted by bats and owls. The Gothic landscape had become *actual*, not imaginary. But it fed the imagination. At the same time, in political and religious terms, Classical Rome was becoming identified with Catholic Rome and the Reformation as a God-driven victory of the Germanic people over Roman decadence. Gothic was soon being considered as a positive when used to refer to a democratic people's opposition to autocratic monarchy. In Whig rhetoric, Gothic stood for freedom and liberty.

The Gothic was a mind-set evident even in garden design. By the middle of the eighteenth century there were *ruined* priories and hermitages to be seen everywhere and in many cases it was a deliberate political statement. The rigid formality of French gardens, epitomized by Versailles, was equated with despotic authority. In England, straight lines were replaced by meandering paths and the picturesque irregularities of nature were viewed as symbols of liberty.

Not everyone could be expected to favour such developments and William Whitehead, the now forgotten Poet Laureate of the day, declared that Gothic, 'allows everyone the privilege of playing the fool and making himself ridiculous in whichever way he pleases.' But this was a minority voice. Gothic was influencing almost every aspect of eighteenth-century life. But to say there was a Gothic revival is something of an overstatement. It had occasionally been comatose, but it had never actually died. It was certainly given a new shot of adrenalin in 1747, however, when Horace Walpole, whose father had built the grandiose Palladian Houghton Hall, purchased the lease of that little Twickenham cottage and began its transformation.

There were times when it seemed less of a building project than a scripted dramatic performance, the central protagonist being the house itself. But as all dramas are illusions, so were the battlements and towers of Strawberry Hill, constructed not of stone, as they might appear, but of wood and plaster, and indoors *trempe l'oeil* wallpaper would be waiting to deceive the visitor. It was less a matter of choice than economy; Horace simply could not afford stone.

In 1750, writing from Arlington Street to Horace Mann in Florence, he casually adds in a PS to a long letter:

> My Dear Sir, I must trouble you with a commission which I don't know whether you can execute. I am going to build a little Gothic Castle at Strawberry Hill. If you can pick up any fragments of old painted glass, arms or anything, I should be extremely obliged to you. I can't say I remember any such thing in Italy, but out of old chateaus I imagine one might get it cheap, if there is any.

No one would think of Horace Walpole as a religious man – at best a sort of comfortable deist – but he does seem to have been fascinated by the trappings of religion. His fascination with Roman Catholicism was, as we have seen, evident during his stay in Italy, when he was so disappointed not to have been in Rome when a new Pope was elected. No religious services were ever held in the Strawberry Hill chapel, yet in it there was the bust of an angel, a bronze crucifix and a censor also in bronze and a 'holy-water-pot of earthen-ware.' The paraphernalia, one might say, was there, but its purpose was to provide another space where he could display new acquisitions, and intended to provide a climax to the garden stroll. One was a stained-glass window from Bexhill with the portraits of Henry III and his Queen, which Walpole believed were among the earliest examples of such glass in England. Another was a cosmati-work shrine which had once graced the church of Santa Maria Maggiore in Rome.

When we think of the Chapel, the thatched cottage and the shell-shaped seat, it is not unreasonable to look upon Walpole as a man who gave orders which others carried out, yet in a quite astonishing letter to Montagu he shows a real depth of garden knowledge. Montagu had asked him for some advice on where to buy trees, which Walpole gave and then declared that he himself had a small nursery, and went on to show that he not only knew what he had in stock, but in what quantities, and even how the plants should be cared for. Another instance, it would seem, of the appearance being a camouflage for a man of ability. Certainly in this case, an ability unusual for someone of his class and social position.

Hands-on work inside the house would have been quite out of the question, but he was sensible enough to realise that his own ideas needed to be tested out somewhere before being put into practice – hence what has come to be known as The Strawberry Hill 'Committee of Taste', whose chief members were John Chute and Richard Bentley.

The Chutes were long-established landed gentry, their family home being The Vyne, a famously beautiful Tudor house near Basingstoke in Hampshire, but which John, being a younger son, did not inherit until he was in his fifties. He was, however, bequeathed an allowance which enabled him to live without actually having to follow any kind of profession. Other than that he too was an Etonian, we know little or nothing about him until the age of forty, when he was invited to accompany his young cousin Francis Whithed on his Grand Tour. They must have made an odd couple. Francis was a sickly youth, almost deaf and probably suffering already from tuberculosis. Chute's health was hardly any better and he suffered from poor eyesight. On top of this he was a martyr to gout, which he sought to alleviate by the curious diet of milk and turnips, though he did later change it to one of ravioli and spinach tarts. Horace referred to them as the Chutheds. Both were decidedly effeminate, but John, with his receding chin, high voice and mincing gait, was really high camp and often to be seen flourishing a fan. When they met in Florence, he and Walpole became lasting friends. Chute had his own room in Strawberry Hill and Horace records that they could sit together for hours without the necessity of talking. Chute was a man of great taste and an accomplished designer. What he meant to Horace and what he contributed to Strawberry Hill can be seen in the letter Horace wrote to Mann in 1776 when Chute died at the age of 73. The letter is a heartfelt encomium running to six handwritten pages:

> Mr Chute and I agreed invariably in our principles; he was my counsel in my affairs, was my oracle in taste, the standard to which I submitted my trifles, and the genius that presided over poor Strawberry. His sense decided me in everything, his wit and quickness illuminated everything. I saw him oftener than any man; to him in every difficulty I had recourse, and him I loved to have here, as our friendship was so entire.

Richard Bentley, son of the renowned classicist and Master of Trinity, was the despair of his father, who failed to recognise that while he had inherited little of his great intellect, his son had real abilities, albeit of a very different nature. Initially he did try to do his best for him, awarding him a Trinity Fellowship and then appointing him Keeper of the King's Library with a stipend of £200 a year when he was only 16. But little went right for him; the disastrous fire of 1731 which destroyed much of the Cottonian collection was laid in part to his negligence and father and son eventually fell out over his extravagance and irresponsibility, with the result that while his sister inherited all their father's money and his cousin his extensive library, Richard was left with nothing. However, on top of his accomplishments as a draughtsman, illustrator, and water-colourist, he became recognised as one of the greatest designers of his day, especially in his design of furniture. Now, when we visit Strawberry Hill, his chairs are what catch the eye and which we would like to carry off home with us if no one was looking.

He was introduced to Horace in 1750 by George Montagu, to whom he wrote in June 1750 to say, 'Mr Bentley has more sense, judgement and wit, more taste and more misfortune than are met in any man.' One of these misfortunes seems to have been his wife, who was not only a bad-tempered harridan, but constantly squandered money they did not have. This was not helped by him regularly getting her pregnant and debt drove them and their ten children to decamp for some time to Jersey where they were out of the reach of their creditors. Eventually, according to William Cole, it was the very existence of Mrs Bentley which caused the lasting breach in the friendship; her husband having being so 'forward as to introduce his wife at his house when people of the first fashion were there, which he thought ill-judged.' But Walpole ensured that he kept his sinecure of £100 and gave frequent financial support to his children.

When Mann received word in 1750 that Horace was going to build a 'little gothic Castle at Strawberry Hill', it is hard to judge what his initial reaction would have been. Such a suggestion was not the revolutionary, forward-looking idea it has sometimes been taken for. It was not the first step on the way to the design of St Pancras Station. In an article in the trend-setting magazine *The*

World of 1753, William Whitehead dismissed Gothic as 'unworthy of the name of Taste' and asserted that fashionable people, 'have long since adopted the Chinese Taste.' Gothic had seemingly become decidedly *unfashionable*. Whitehead went on, 'A few years ago, everything was Gothic; our houses, our beds, our books, our couches were all copied from some part or other of our old cathedrals.' It was now looked down upon as something more befitting 'the middling sort'. It was to be seen in little summer-houses and in follies – hermitages being among the favourites. There was even a DIY Gothic manual, *Gothic Architecture improved by rules and proportion* published by Batty Langley in the very same year that Horace acquired Strawberry Hill. In it Langley sought to identify Gothic architecture on the model of the five Vitruvian orders of Classical architecture, but these and his *rules* were largely of his own invention. It was very influential, but in the closing pages of *Anecdotes on Painting* Horace gives it short shrift: 'All that his books achieved, has been to teach carpenters to massacre that venerable species, and to give occasion to those who know nothing of the matter, to mistake his clumsy efforts for real imitations.'

The Committee of Taste were careful to go back to and consult original Gothic works and designs, and in the correspondence with William Cole we see how many they consulted and how carefully. Of particular interest is his letter of 11 August 1769 in which he considers the possibility of writing a history of Gothic architecture. It never progressed further than a possibility, but even at this stage the seriousness with which he takes it is remarkable for its detail. He even envisaged including 'The prices and wages of workmen and the comparative value of money and provisions at the several periods should be stated as far as it is possible to get materials.' It was this professionalism of approach, together with Walpole's social position and reputation as an arbiter of Taste, which encouraged society to feel that there might be something in it and re-established the true Gothic. And yet, writing to Miss Mary Berry three years before his death he said that ' ... every true Goth must perceive that they [my rooms] are more the works of fancy than imitation.'

Strawberry Hill was to become the project of a lifetime for Horace. Changes and extensions to the building continued right up until 1790, by which time a little china closet which measured 10' X 12' had been replaced by a gallery 56' X 15'. The 14' long Little Cloister had become The Great Cloister and was all of 56' long. In the first phase, between 1750 and 1756, the bijou little building was enclosed in a Gothic shell and he concentrated on the private rooms, then came the Library and the Great Parlour. In 1761 truly major undertakings began: the Great West Wing was added featuring the Long Gallery, The Round Tower and the Great North Bedchamber. These new additions almost doubled the size of what had previously been a compact, squarish house, turning it into a straggling succession of state rooms intended for entertaining and display. In 1771 we find him telling Mann, 'You must know that the little villa is grown into a superb castle.'

He needed space to show to advantage his growing collection. In 1762 he had confessed to Montagu:

> I begin to be ashamed of my magnificence; Strawberry is growing sumptuous in its latter day; it will scarce be any longer like the

fruit of its name or the modesty of its demeanour ... In truth my collection was too great already to be lodged humbly, it had extended my walls and pomp followed.

Over the years he had never ceased collecting: paintings, things of beauty and things of value, but also objects which evoked for him some feeling or conjured up some personal association. The sheer variety is astonishing; one of the oddest items being Cardinal Wolsey's hat. But a postscript to a letter to Henry Conway of February 1756 shows that he came very close to acquiring another unusual piece of headwear to go alongside it: 'I forgot that I was outbid for Oliver Cromwell's nightcap.'

Horace once defined a museum as, 'an hospital for everything that is singular, whether the thing has acquired singularity from having escaped the ravages of time, from any natural oddness in itself, or from being so insignificant that nobody ever thought it worth the while to produce any more of the same sort.' There is a certain charm about that last statement. And writing to Mann he said, 'You can't think what a closet I have filled up! Such a mixture of French gaiety and Roman vertu.' By the time of his death in 1797 the collection featured at least 4,000 objects, together with thousands of prints, paintings and drawings. When the time came for it to be dispersed in 1842, the sale took 32 days to be completed. So varied were the items, they have been called 'indiscriminate clutter' and were satirised in *The Times,* where it was suggested that the collection even featured such rarities as 'the bridge of the fiddle on which Nero played while Rome was burning.' Nevertheless, the illustrated catalogue itself was such a success that it ran into eight editions and the final total raised amounted to £33,000.

The collection and the curiosity value of the building itself had from early on attracted visitors in such numbers that a degree of organisation soon became necessary. Here we see a practical side to Horace's nature which is very far removed from the dilettante façade he sometimes assumed. He issued tickets. Not only that; he had leaflets printed informing people where and when such tickets could be obtained and what the conditions of entry were. These leaflets he then arranged to have distributed in bookshops and other likely venues around the city. Getting a ticket was simple: application was to be made in advance to his house in Berkeley Square and, perhaps rather surprisingly, it stated that no one who applied would be refused. But there were conditions. Groups were limited to four persons and only one group per day. No visitors would be admitted between 1 May and 1 October, and visits could only be made between twelve and three and the house would never 'be shown after dinner.' And the final condition was, very wisely, 'Those who have Tickets are desired not to bring children.'

At the outset, this opportunity to share his love of the house was a joy, and to have been shown round it by Horace himself and to have heard his stories of what things were and where they came from must have been an unforgettable experience, but as its popularity grew so did the number of visitors and the joy began to pall. His memorandum book recording visitors from 1784 - 1796 totals some 80 groups per season (May to early October) and as there were usually four in each group this amounts to close on 4000 people walking through his house in the last 13 years of his life. It proved to be too much and he had been regretting his decision long before that as we learn from a letter to Montagu in September 1763.

> My house is full of people and has been so from the instant I breakfasted and more are coming – in short I keep an inn, the sign, The Gothic Castle – since my gallery was finished, I have not been in it a quarter of an hour together; my whole time is passed in giving tickets for seeing it and hiding myself while it is seen – take my advice, never build a charming house between London and Hampton Court, everybody will live in it but you.

There were some visitors even less welcome than children, but far harder to keep out. The battlements and pinnacles may have looked like stonework but were mostly made of wood and such decoration 'provoked the wanton malice of the lower classes', who broke them off almost as soon as they were put up, but Horace, we are told, bore it with great patience. He must have been building for posterity, Mary Berry said, as he had outlived three of his battlements.

Visitors were never given a free run of the house of course. Horace had decided which rooms could be seen and in what order, and they were guided on their tour, chiefly by his housekeeper, Margaret Young. At the end of their tour, there was an opportunity to have a dish of tea in the chapel and also to take away with them, as a memento, a print of one of the water colours of the house. It would seem that Horace had, single-handedly, invented the whole stately home visiting experience: tickets, guided tours, plus the gift shop and the café, but with one significant difference – these visits were free. But then organisation went even one step further: he invented the guide book. Wanting to be certain that Mrs Young gave them exactly the right information, he produced a little book in 1774, chiefly intended for his servants' use, but then in 1784 he published, on his own press, a substantial volume,

A Description of the Villa of Mr Horace Walpole at Strawberry Hill near Twickenham. It is an extremely attractive book, its title page decorated with a delicately coloured frieze of honeysuckle and (of course) strawberries and with 27 full-page engravings. It would have been a memento to treasure. Indeed, on his death he left 80 copies as gifts for friends.

Running to over 130 pages, the *Description* is a meticulous and masterly piece of work which must have taken hours of research and compilation to bring to completion. It is the work of a professional and here again is the familiar dilemma; a dilemma which is immediately evident in The Preface. Its opening words are, 'It will look, I fear, a little like arrogance in a private man to give a printed description of his villa and collection.' Again he is anxious about what people will think of him. Will it make him appear ridiculous? A recurrent fear. But there is not a thread of vanity in what he had been working on for so long. What has been on his mind, and his driving force, were the events of 1774, when his lunatic nephew sold all Sir Robert's paintings to the Empress of Russia – 'Having lived, unhappily, to see the noblest school of painting that this kingdom beheld, transported almost out of the sight of Europe ... ' He knows that a time will come when his own collection will be broken up, but he is now prepared for it – 'Far from such visions of self-love, the following account of pictures and rarities is given with a view to their future dispersion. The several purchasers will find a history of their purchases; nor do virtuosos dislike to refer to such a catalogue for an authentic certificate of their curiosities.' He is thinking ahead, thinking of the wider world of scholars and collectors and seeking to establish Strawberry Hill in that context. Of course he was right to do so; it has proved to be invaluable in the recent efforts to bring together again some of the treasures and art works he once had around him. The *Description* was never intended to be a work to be read, but dipping into it after a visit brings back memories of the house and its glories.

The Tour had to it something of a theatrical performance. At its start everything is closed in and small as visitors were first confined to a little waiting room and invited to inspect a china closet crammed with almost 700 rare and beautiful items. Then an inauspicious little door opened and they found themselves in the Great Parlour, a room 12 feet high and 30 feet long. The eye is caught by a flamboyant Gothic chimney piece designed by Richard Bentley, and along the walls are eight black chairs – again Bentley's design – the design of their backs being based on the framework of Gothic church windows. The walls were hung with portraits of family and friends: both his parents, his father's second wife, and brothers, sisters, nieces and nephews, but with pride of place going to Reynolds' outstandingly beautiful portrait, 'The Three Ladies Waldegrave'. After the *gloomth* (Horace's own splendid neologism) of the waiting room, the Great Parlour is bright and cheerful, reminding us that he once observed, ' ... in truth, I did not mean to make my house so Gothic as to exclude convenience, and modern refinements in luxury. The designs of the inside and outside are strictly ancient, but the decorations are modern.' And comfortable and modern they were. The carpets were Axminster and Wilton and the Breakfast Room he describes as 'hung with a blue and white paper in stripes adorned with festoons, and a thousand plump chairs, couches and luxurious settees covered with linen of the same pattern.' Something no doubt of an exaggeration as to number, but we take the point.

Gloomth prevailed once more in the narrow Gothic – Bentley's design again – staircase which leads to the first floor. In the long account of the house which he sent to Horace Mann in June 1753 we read ' ... you come to the hall and staircase, which it is impossible to describe to you, as it is the most particular and chief beauty of the castle.' In a little vestibule at the top there is a display of 'old coats of mail, Indian shields made of rhinoceros's hides, broadswords, quivers, long bows, arrows and spears.' He told Mann they 'were all *supposed* to have been taken by one of his ancestors Sir Terry Robsart in the Holy Wars, but his italics show that authenticity was not always a major concern. He referred to it as *The Armoury* and indeed at the top of the staircase was a suit of armour he acquired in 1771 with help of Mme du Deffand and which he believed (erroneously it is now thought) to have belonged to Francis I of France. It would, we can be sure, have enthralled those visitors who had read *Otranto*. Authenticity always played second fiddle to *atmosphere*. As he said in the Preface to his *Description of the Villa* 'I do not mean to defend by argument a small capricious house. It was built to please my own taste, and in sole degree to realize my own vision.'

In contrast there then comes a series of compact little rooms which glow with colour, rooms which must have been positively cosy to live in. There was an Arcadian feel to these rooms; their colours reflecting and harmonising with the garden and the river they looked out onto. The Blue Breakfast Room was Horace's favourite. As well as those 'couches and luxurious settees', he described it to Mann as having:

a bow-window commanding the prospect, and gloomed with limes that shade half each window, already darkened with painted glass in chiaroscuro, set in deep blue glass.

The blue glass being of the most beautiful Flemish roundels. This room was where Horace and his friends sat to take breakfast along with a number of pet spaniels, and joined at times, we are told, by a red squirrel which boldly came in through the window.

Smaller than the Blue Breakfast Room, yet still containing 141 pictures, was the Green Closet. Green being regarded as a restful colour, this was where Horace did most of his writing and where the Committee of Taste would meet to plan their next project. The *Description* begins 'In the windows are some very curious pieces of painted glass', which is something of an understatement, as these *pieces,* featuring birds and flowers and painted in the 16th and 17th century, are among the most beautiful in the whole house.

The next stop on the Tour, after these compact little domestic rooms, is The Library, a room no bibliophile can take more than two steps into without standing there, stunned. It contained some 8,000 volumes, yet Horace was not what we would consider a book collector. He bought books to be read and many have his own handwritten comments in the margin. It is very much a working library, enabling him to follow his very professional interests in the arts and antiquities.

Designed largely by John Chute, the library was completed in 1754 and of all the rooms in the house is the most fully realised in the Gothic style. At the further end a large window gave onto a view of the lawns and the Thames while every other wall contained a range of bookshelves broken only by a chimney-piece based on two famous Gothic tombs: Clarence's stone tomb in Canterbury Cathedral and that of John of Eltham in Westminster Abbey. Chute, who had been brought up in a house of medieval origin and so understood Gothic at first hand, always sought historical accuracy rather than fantasy, hence basing his designs for these bookcases on an engraving of the arched side-doors into the Choir of Old St Paul's. Ingeniously, the arches, made in a tracery of lime wood and painted to look like stone, could be swung out on hinges to give access to those books which were behind the elaborate carvings of the upper part of the cases.

Although Gothic, there is a kind of exuberance about these shelves in the way that they go soaring up to the ceiling. And what a ceiling. Designed by Horace himself, it is a celebration of his family's ancestry. In the centre is the Walpole shield glowing in gold and around it the quarters borne by the family and of all the other families by whom they had been allied in marriage. It is a magnificent expression of family pride.

Nevertheless, splendid though it is, it is outdone in every way by the ceiling of the Great gallery. 'Richer than the roof of paradise' is how Horace described it to Thomas Mason. Entering this glittering Gallery – 17' high and 56' x 13' – after the grave solemnity of the Holbein Chamber is a truly theatrical performance and intentionally so.

Bentley had drawn up the initial designs for the Gallery, but Horace found them too tame and that was the end of their collaboration. Instead, a new member joined the Committee, Thomas Pitt, nephew of William Pitt the Elder. Mrs Thrale described him as 'a finical ladylike man,' but in Horace's view he was, 'very amiable and very sensible, and one of the very few that

I reckon quite worthy of being at home in Strawberry.' On his Grand Tour Thomas had visited Spain and acquired a love of Moorish architecture, probably from the Alhambra, and it is to him that we owe some of the room's overall flamboyance, though nothing was ever done without Horace's say-so, as he told Montagu, 'I do not love to trust a hammer or a brush without my own supervisal.'

It is hard to take one's eyes off the glorious gold and white fan-vaulted ceiling, based, Horace said, on Henry VII's Chapel at Westminster, but clearly with fond memories of King's College Chapel too. But if it is hard to takes one's eyes off it, it is even harder to believe that what you are looking at is not stone but papier maché. So much of Strawberry Hill, like its owner, is not what it would first seem.

The Gallery is flooded with light coming in from five large south-facing windows which give a view onto the Thames; a light which is picked up by mirrors set into embrasures in the opposite wall, embrasures themselves partly covered by a gold filigree network and backed by a majestic crimson damask wall-hanging. The walls again support a medley of pictures, one of the most interesting being Van Somer's *Henry Carey, Lord Falkland*, a portrait which was to feature so significantly and spookily in *The Castle of Otranto*. And in pride of place there stood the bronze Boccapudugli Eagle which he had been at such pains and such expense to purchase in Florence.

Everywhere is flamboyance and extravagance. This was a place meant to entertain and to impress. In his letter to Montagu he said, 'I begin to be ashamed of my magnificence. Strawberry is growing sumptuous in its later days.' But of course he was not at all ashamed; he gloried in it, as is evident from an account he wrote to Mann of an entertainment given in October 1778 for the three ladies Waldegrave: Maria, Laura and Horatia. It was an entertainment in which Kitty Clive, the actress, descended from the Gallery ceiling on a swing, lit by a spot of moonlight! He admits that:

> the entertainment given by the Queen of the Amazons to the King of Mauritania in the Castle of Ice and the Ball made for the Princess of Persia by the Duke of Sparta in the Salon of Roses were both of them more delightful

But claims that:

> ... the illumination of the Gallery surpassed the Palace of the Sun; and when its fretted ceiling, which you know is richer than the roof of paradise, opened for the descent of Mrs Clive in the full moon, nothing could be more striking.

And Kitty Clive was 68 years old when she made this spectacular performance; a truly remarkable woman. She had begun her career as a singer, taking the role of Delilah in Handel's *Samson,* but on joining Garrick's company at Drury Lane she quickly established a reputation as the leading comedy actress of her time, famous for her boisterous performances and for her laugh. Horace was a great admirer of her – another of his unlikely friendships – and when she retired from the theatre in 1755, he gave her a cottage which became known as Little Strawberry Hill. There she stayed until her death in 1785 when he wrote an epitaph for her which can still be seen in St Mary's church in Twickenham.

> Ye smiles and jests still hover round,
> This is mirth's consecrated ground.
> Here lived the laughter-loving dame,
> A matchless actress, Clive her name.
> The comic muse with her retired
> And shed a tear when she expired.

It is hard to do justice to Strawberry Hill, to describe it or even to account for it. Its blend of grandeur, beauty and bizarre eccentricity is unparalleled and it is best left to Horace himself to explain it, as he did in the closing of his *Preface*:

> But I do not mean to defend by argument a small capricious house. It was built to please my own taste, and in some degree to realize my own visions. I have specified what it contains: could I describe the gay but tranquil scene where it stands, and add the beauty of the landscape to the romantic cast of the mansion, it would raise more pleasing sensations than a dry list of curiosities can excite; at least the prospect would recall the good humour of those who might be disposed to condemn the fantastic fabric and to think it a very proper habitation of, as it was the scene that inspired, the author of the Castle of Otranto.

When Horace died in 1797 he left Anne Damer, the daughter of his cousin and close friend Henry Conway, a lifetime tenancy of Strawberry Hill and a £2000 annuity towards its upkeep. A sculptress of some repute who had been commissioned to sculpt the heads of Thames and Isis for the new bridge at Henley, she continued her work there. She also revived the Strawberry Hill Press. A description of the house in a guidebook of 1800 shows that it was still attracting visitors.

The approach to the house, through a grove of lofty trees, the embattled walls, overgrown with ivy, the spirey pinnacles and gloomy cast of the buildings give it the air of an ancient abbey and fill the beholder with awe.

But in 1810, on the death of her mother, Lady Ailesbury, who had been living there with her, Anne decided that it was more than she could cope with and passed it on to the Waldegrave family. It was then that neglect began to take its toll, especially under the 7th Earl Waldegrave, a total wastrel who served a six-month prison sentence for 'riotous behaviour' after drunkenly assaulting a policeman. Heavily in debt, it was he who sold off the entire contents of the house in the great sale of 1842. Fortunately he died not long after and his widow, Frances Braham, a society beauty, married into money – twice – and began extensive alterations, but they were alterations so out of keeping with any of Horace's designs: a grand dining room, a billiards room, even a ballroom and a new wing for guest bedrooms. She even had the sparkling white outside covered over in cement. Nor did the garden escape her attentions, acquiring a fountain and a maze. It fills one with horror, but it was her house and suited her life style.

On her death in 1879, the house was sold to a wealthy banker, Baron de Stern, and remained in his family until 1923, when it was bought by the Catholic Education Council for use as a Teacher Training College. They did their best to maintain and protect it, but it was not enough. It had reached a stage where only drastic action could save it and in 2000 the Strawberry Hill Trust was founded and granted a long lease. The restoration work they undertook has since succeeded beyond all expectations. With grants totalling £10 Million from the Heritage Lottery Fund, the

World Memorial Fund and English Heritage, Strawberry Hill reopened to the public in 2015. Frances Braham's excrescences had all been cleared away along with her cement so the house now stands out again in all the white of its 'wedding cake' glory and the rooms restored in such a way that it seems Horace has just popped out for a while and will be back soon to conduct us all on a tour. Ah, but it's a pardonable fantasy, as Henry James once put it.

5

RECONCILIATION

FIVE YEARS PASSED BETWEEN THE QUARREL at Reggio and the reconciliation in 1745 between Walpole and Gray. It is by no means certain who it was who persuaded Horace that the time was now right to suggest that Gray might visit him in Arlington Street. We know it was a lady, and high in the list of possibles is Mrs Francis Chute, the sister-in-law of John Chute, who loved both men and must have found the situation very trying. If she was indeed the lady trusted with what was a delicate situation, she succeeded and the meeting was arranged. But the initial encounter did not go well. Gray always found it difficult to swallow his pride and even after their reconciliation, Horace agreed with George Montagu:

> I agree absolutely with you in your opinion about Gray, he is the worst company in the world. From a melancholy turn, from living reclusely, and from a little too much dignity, he never converses easily; all his words are measured and chosen, and formed into sentences; his writings are admirable; he himself is not agreeable.

Gray, it would seem, stood a little too much on his dignity and made no real effort to ease the situation. In a letter to Thomas Wharton recounting, albeit briefly, all that happened on that occasion he openly states, 'I took my leave very indifferently.' Horace was, it appears, far more effusive in his welcome than Gray had anticipated or was comfortable with. He had kissed him on both cheeks, 'with all the ease of one who receives an acquaintance just come out of the country.' He then sat him down and chatted away for three hours 'about this & that & t'other.' That was probably a deliberate and very shrewd ploy on Horace's part. To make any reference to the past, certainly to any cause of their rift, would only have brought about an even more stilted awkwardness. Their meeting the following night was even more shrewd. Ashton was present. By this time, Horace and Gray would both have recognised him for the toady he was and having a common enemy brought about the beginnings of an alliance. That was all that was needed and he tells Wharton, 'Next morning I breakfasted with Mr W. when we had all the Éclaircissement I ever expected and left him better satisfied than I had ever been hitherto.' The tone suggests he still felt himself to be in the right, but their friendship – with a little more reserve perhaps – continued until Gray's death in 1771.

As for Ashton, it was the beginning of the end for him. He had, as Gray puts it, the foolishness 'to be angry about the letter I wrote him', almost admitting his guilt in doing so. Then on their way home in a coach together, Ashton, 'opened his heart' leaving Gray 'with still less reason to have a good opinion of him than (if possible) I ever had before.' When the end came, it was abrupt. There had always been something about Ashton which suggested that he was primarily interested in himself and what he could get for himself. And he had indeed done well, a fellowship at Eton and an excellent living at Aldingham.

But in a letter of 25th July 1750 to Mann, Horace refers to him as:

> ... a clergyman, who, in one word, has had great preferments, and owes everything on earth to me. I have long had reason to complain of his behaviour, in short my father is dead, and I can make no bishops. He has at last quite thrown off his mask and in the most direct manner, against my will, has written against my friend Dr Middleton. I have forbid him my house. [Ashton had been staying at Arlington Street for some considerable time.] I own it very pleasant t'other day on meeting Mr Tonson his bookseller and asking him if he had sold many of Mr Ashton's books, to be told 'Very few indeed, Sir!'

It is a pleasure we share with him, I think. His Old Etonian friend is now simply 'a clergyman'. This is a side of Horace we do not often see and it is worth bearing in mind that while he has frequently been called effeminate, he did not suffer fools gladly, nor disloyalty, and when the need arose he knew how to put such people in their place.

With our attention focused so closely on Walpole and Gray, it comes as something of a jolt to realise that the year of their reconciliation, 1745, was also the year of the Jacobite Invasion. It is curious the way this violent insurrection has dwindled in the popular imagination into something approaching a costume drama, a romantic adventure featuring bearded Highlanders in kilts engaged in an enterprise which somehow *ganged agley*. It has become glamourized into a tale of Bonnie Prince Charlie and Flora Macdonald, played out against a background chorus of 'Over the sea to Skye'. And the hero of this adventure, the Bonnie Prince, is celebrated not only for failing, but then for running away and leaving his followers to face the brutal and bloody consequences of his own foolish ambitions. Flora and her husband, who could have earned a fortune by betraying him, were soon so destitute that they joined the mass emigration to America, but even that failed and they returned to a life of poverty, while Charlie seems to have forgotten all about her and drunkenly idled away his life in Rome.

The reality was indeed far from romantic and in Horace's letters to Mann in Florence we are witness to events as they were taking place. This is what makes them so fascinating. Normally all history is hindsight coloured by whatever present time it is being written in. It records events which have finished. But Horace did not know then that it would all fail and that the Bonnie Prince would be spirited away. On the contrary, in the early stages, and particularly after the rout at Prestonpans, it looked as though the Scottish rebels would be victorious; and victory, one has to realise, would have meant the overthrow of the House of Hanover and the re-establishment of a Stuart, Roman Catholic monarchy. It is hard to imagine such a situation, but one thing is certain: it would not have been pretty. Even in Horace's fairly light-hearted account of the conclusive Battle of Culloden we are given a shocking reminder of what hand-to-hand warfare was like: 'They killed Lord Robert Kerr, a handsome young gentleman, who was cut to pieces with above thirty wounds.'

But there is nothing light-hearted about his initial accounts. In the first week of September he is already saying, 'I look upon Scotland as gone!' One can sense the growing anxiety. Within a very short time it was clear that they had underestimated the Highlanders: 'However, we are convinced that they are not such raw ragamuffins as they were represented.' English losses were heavy, 'Our dragoons most shamefully fled without striking a blow' and 'We have lost all our artillery, five hundred men taken – and *three* killed and several officers ... This defeat has frightened everybody.' The result was on a knife edge, ' ... if they come into England, another battle, with no advantage on our side, may determine our fate.' The *Boy*, as he was referred to in his first letters to Mann, is now *The Prince*. There was also the fear that 'One can't tell what assurances of support they may have from the Jacobites in England.' A *fifth column* was always a dangerous possibility and as in all such situations there were rumours of atrocities, 'At Edinburgh and thereabouts they commit the most horrid barbarities.' Some English prisoners had almost certainly been murdered.

And what were the English politicians doing? Seeking to use the situation to enhance their own political standing is one answer. Lord Granville, Horace tells Mann, persisted in telling the King that it was an affair of no consequence and the Duke of Newcastle was glad of any rebel victory as it allowed him to confute Lord Granville, especially in the eyes of the King. And Pitt's solution was to augment the country's naval force as being the only method of putting an end to the rebellion. As Horace scornfully put it, 'Ships built a year hence to suppress an army of Highlanders now marching through England.'

Marching through England they were. The City of Carlisle, having tried to hold out, had fallen: ' ... the next day the rebels returned, having placed the women and children of the country in waggons in front of their army, and forcing the peasants to fix the scaling-ladders.' A callous manoeuvre and one which was to be repeated in many a subsequent war.

Then came the surprising retreat from Derby: 'It is said they have left all their cannon behind them, and twenty waggons of sick ... we dread them no longer.' That was written in December 1745, but the decisive battle of Culloden did not take place until April 16th of the following year. 'They have lost above a thousand men in the engagement and pursuit,' he tells Mann; despite, ' ... the whole engagement not lasting above a quarter of an hour.' London was now celebrating: 'The town is all blazing round me, as I write, with fireworks and illuminations'. He concludes his letter to Mann wondering whether or not to send him half a dozen sky-rockets so that he can join in the fun.

But after the celebrations, there followed the recriminations: the trial and execution of the rebel lords. The two letters relating these events are among the most eloquent and most quoted of all Walpole's letters. The first, to Horace Mann is dated 1 August 1746, and begins with a moving solemnity: 'I am this moment come from the conclusion of the greatest and most melancholy scene I ever yet saw! you will easily guess it was the Trials of the Rebel Lords.'

One of the most distinctive qualities of these letters is that although they are addressed to Mann, they read as though they are addressed to us as well, and to us as individuals. As he once wrote to George Montagu, 'I shall relate it to you to show you the manners of the age, which are always as entertaining to a person fifty miles off as to one born an hundred and fifty years after the time.' More years than that have now passed and still we are gripped by what we read.

The variety of approaches he adopts is another of his strengths.

The sequence of events is given to us as a narrative, but there is also a dramatic element to it. Characters are described to us physically and we are told what they wear, how they hold themselves, how they move and we hear what they had to say. There is even, despite the solemnity of the occasion, a little touch of humour which adds to the humanity.

There were three lords standing trial: the Lords Kilmarnock, Cromartie and Balmerino. Their first appearance in the court, Horace declares, 'shocked me! their behaviour melted me!' Lord Kilmarnock impressed him immediately: ' ... tall and slender, with an extreme fine person; his behaviour a most just mixture between dignity and submission.' In contrast, the Lord High Steward – Lord Hardwicke – comes in for some harsh criticism: ' ... he was peevish and instead of keeping to the humane dignity of the Law of England, whose character is to point out favour to the criminal, he crossed them, and almost scolded at any offer they made towards defence.'

When we encounter Lord Balmerino it is very easy to see whose side Horace is on. If the Lord High Sheriff was 'peevish', the Solicitor General is *officious* and *insolent* when he addresses Balmerino. Horace, it would seem, is not as interested in the treason, the politics or the legality of the event as the *humanity* of it. Lord Balmerino is presented to us as being quite endearing: ' ... he is the most natural brave old fellow I ever saw; the highest intrepidity, even to indifference. At the bar he behaved like a soldier and a man; in the intervals of form, with carelessness and humour.'

When the prisoners were brought from The Tower in separate coaches, there was some dispute as to which one the axe should go in. 'Come, come,' said Balmerino, 'put it with me.' And that settled it. 'The old hero,' as Horace called him, shook hands with the witnesses and explained that one of his reasons for pleading Not Guilty was that so many ladies might not be disappointed of their show. And if George Budd's drawing of the execution is a fair representation, then the crowd would have been numbered in thousands. The lords were all found guilty of course, but pleas were made to the King to spare their lives. The Duke of Cumberland, as was only to be expected, opposed any such suggestion and had his way. The letter to Mann ends, 'It was lately proposed in the city to present him with the freedom of some company; and one of the aldermen said aloud; then let it be of *the butchers*.' And Butcher Cumberland is how we know him. That is the kind of history we need.

The letter relating the executions is dated three weeks later and the detail – though it is second hand as Horace himself was not there – is disturbing. Lord Kilmarnock:

> ... with great composure, and after some trouble put on a napkin-cap, and then several times tried the block, the executioner, who was in white, out of tenderness concealing the axe behind himself. At last the Earl knelt down, with a visible unwillingness to depart, and after five minutes dropped his handkerchief, the signal, and his head was cut off at once, only hanging by a bit of skin, and was received in a scarlet cloth by four of the undertaker's men kneeling, who wrapped it up and put it in the coffin with the body; orders having been given not to expose the head, as used to be the custom.

It is one of those oddities of history that 15 years later, Lord Kilmarnock's son, in his capacity as High Constable of Scotland, would attend the Coronation of King George III in the very same hall in which his father had been condemned to the block.

Balmerino was unrepentant to the end, drinking a toast to the health of King James, delivering a treasonous speech and declaring, 'If I had a thousand lives, I would lay them all down in the same cause.' One cannot but admire his sang froid and singleness of mind, nor the way he met his death: 'Being told he was on the wrong side of the block, he vaulted round and immediately gave the signal by tossing up his arm, as if he were giving the signal for battle.' There is so much in that one word *vaulted*.

And just as the letter about the trial had ended with a note of humour, so this concludes, 'As he walked from his prison to execution, seeing every window and top of house filled with spectators, he cried out, 'Look, look, how they are all piled up like rotten oranges!''

Horace's own contribution to the earlier celebrations took what, to us, looks like rather an unexpected turn – a poem: the Epilogue to Nicholas Rowe's play *Tamerlane*, and which was sub-titled for this particular occasion 'On The Suppression of the Rebellion'. From 1702 right up until 1815, Rowe's play was performed on the 4th and 5th of each November, first to celebrate William of Orange's birthday and then his landing at Brixham in 1688 and what was to become known as The Glorious Revolution. In the play Tamur represented William and Bajazet his sworn enemy Louis XIV. But in 1746, when the actress Mrs Prichard spoke the Epilogue at Covent Garden, another William was also being fêted: William Duke of Cumberland, whose victory at Culloden was seen as a double victory in that he had defeated not only the Jacobites but Popery, a triumph therefore both political and religious.

Had Popery succeeded, it would, it was believed, have posed a threat to the freedom of the theatre and this Horace stresses at the outset.

> An equal fate the stage and Britain dreaded,
> Had Rome's young missionary succeeded.

But it is the Duke of Cumberland's victory which is the central theme.

> What youth is he with comeliest conquest crown'd
> His warlike brow with full-blown laurels bound?
> What wreaths are these that victory dares to join
> And blend with trophies of my fav'rite Boyne?
>
> Thou shalt be WILLIAM – like the last design'd
> The tyrants' scourge and blessing of mankind.

While not outstanding, it is an efficient piece of verse, applauded to the echo at both performances and published immediately afterwards, though Horace chose to remain anonymous, as he did later when it was published in Robert Dodsley's definitive anthology *A Collection of Poems by Several Hands* in 1748.

Dodsley led such an astonishing life that a brief digression seems not un-called for. Even Boswell thought that someone ought to have written his biography. Born in Mansfield in 1704, the son of an impecunious schoolmaster, he received only the most basic of educations at his father's free grammar school, leaving there as soon as he was fourteen to be apprenticed to a local stocking-weaver. Wisely, he absconded before his term was up and went off to London where he became a footman, an unlikely and inauspicious start for a man who was to become one of the most important and influential publishers of the century. Innate ability and a powerful business sense – and he clearly had both – would not have been enough at that time to effect such a transformation. He needed to have luck and Dodsley did often find himself in just the right place at the right time.

His first master was Charles Dartineuf, a member of the Kit Cat Club, around whose dining table would have been gathered such men as Addison, Steele and Congreve, as well as Lord Cobham and Sir Robert Walpole, listening to whom would, for Footman Dodsley, have been something of a liberal education in itself. More advantageous still was his subsequent move to the household of the Honourable Mrs Jane Lowther. She was a lady with a passion for literature and was delighted to find that her new employee wrote poetry. This was when Stephen Duck, the thresher poet, was attracting a growing audience and royal patronage, so a London-based footman-bard had an obvious market potential. When his collection 'A Muse in Livery' was published in 1732 she had secured for him a subscription list replete with the names of dukes and duchesses, counts and countesses and innumerable honourables. The book could not help but be a success and emboldened, Dodsley left domestic service to learn the trade of book-selling. He joined Pope's publisher Lawton Gilliver where he learned all aspects of the trade, so that by 1735 he was able to open his own shop, financed by a generous gift of £100 from Alexander Pope himself. Pope had been pleased and impressed by a poem Dodsley had written in praise of him. But his generosity was not entirely selfless; one would hardly expect such a thing of him. Having a publisher indebted to him meant that his works – and the chicanery surrounding the publication of his letters – would be produced exactly as he wanted them. Soon Dodsley was not only the publisher of Pope, but of Gray, Goldsmith, Akenside and of course Samuel Johnson's Dictionary.

Horace had two other poems published in Dodsley's 1748 anthology, 'The Epistle from Florence to Thomas Ashton, Esq.', which, as we have seen, he had written while on his grand tour and 'The Beauties', which again takes the form of an epistle, this time to Mr Eckhardt, a German portrait painter whom Horace had commissioned to paint many of his friends and family. It urges him not to waste his time painting the beauties of ancient Greece, but to favour instead the beauties to be found living in London.

> In Britain's isle observe the fair,
> And curious choose your models there.

They could provide him with a whole gallery of goddesses, he tells him and then proceeds to list the various candidates.

> The crescent on her brow display'd
> In curls of loveliest brown inlaid,
> With every charm to rule the night,
> Like Dian, Strafford woos the sight,
> The graceful shape, the piercing eye,
> The snowy bosom's purity,
> The unaffected gentle phrase
> Of native wit in all she says;
> Eckhardt, for these thy art's too faint:
> You may admire, but cannot paint.

The rhymes click nicely into place and he never puts a metrical foot wrong, but Horace was no poet. It is a lifeless sequence, though no doubt pleasing to the various young ladies of fashion who are all identified in footnotes.

It was written as a kind of thankyou letter to his friend Henry Fox, Secretary of War, with whom he had been staying in London and was intended to amuse his wife, Lady Caroline, hoping that 'it should make her think me a reasonable creature.' He sent it off on 19th July and within three days Fox was thanking him in the most absurdly fulsome terms – 'Upon my word, I never read anything more poetical and pretty' and suggesting that it deserved a wider audience. Horace was appalled at the idea and replied with equal alacrity, ' ... you alarm me with talking of making those I sent you public. I never thought poetry excusable, but in the manner I sent you mine, just to divert anybody one loves for half an hour.' He never did have a high regard for poetry. In this same letter he refers to Thomson as 'a silly fellow' and writing to Mann once declared, 'I cannot bear modern poetry.' But there was another reason why he did not want his verses circulated; the old fear of ridicule, adding ' ... to make anything one writes, especially poetry, public, is giving everybody leave under one's own hand to call one fool.' The poem was circulated and he was not at all pleased, but he had no objection to his work appearing in volume three of Dodsley's anthology, as long as he remained anonymous.

Interestingly, in the second volume are three poems whose author is named. They are the work of Mr Gray and are his three Odes: 'On the Spring', 'On a Distant Prospect of Eton College' and 'On the Death of a Favourite Cat'. For most of his life Gray suffered from bouts of melancholy and depression. When he was only twenty-one, he wrote to Richard West, 'Low spirits are my true and faithful companions. They get up with me, go to bed with me, make journeys and returns as I do ... but most commonly we sit alone together, and are the prettiest insipid company in the world.' But in 1742, the year when he wrote the Eton College poem, he had cause enough to be in low spirits. When he had come back to England the year before, he had not liked what he found. 'If this be London, Lord send me to Constantinople,' he had written to Chute. As no kind of profession had any appeal for him, he had returned to Peterhouse, but was not happy there, indeed he was tormented there as we have seen. In 1741 his father died and while they had never enjoyed any kind of relationship, his death, which was slow and painful, occasioned a complex series of financial problems. Added to this he was lonely. His reconciliation with Walpole was still some years way, and then in June 1742 his closest friend Richard West died. What made it worse was that no one told him he had died. He learned of it by coming across some obituary verses – written by Ashton – in the *London Magazine.* The 'Ode to Spring' had been written at West's request and the manuscript is headed 'At Stoke, the beginning of June 1742 to Favonius, not knowing he was then dead.' It was a loss Gray felt deeply. He wrote a 'Sonnet: on the Death of Richard West' which he never published. It was such a show of emotion - 'My lonely Anguish melts no Heart, but mine' – which he rarely allowed himself. The sonnet was written in early August and a few days later he wrote 'On a Distant Prospect of Eton College'. From Stoke Poges at that time it was still possible to look over towards Eton and Windsor and catch a glimpse of the spires and towers, but the word *Distant* here also refers to time. He is looking back to his days there as a pupil and the happiness he had known as a member of the *Quadruple Alliance.* These stanzas are not, however, simply another case of *happiest-days-of-your-life* nostalgia. The Etonians who are 'Disporting on thy margent green'

> Still as they run they look behind
> They hear a voice in every wind
> And snatch a fearful joy.

Nevertheless, as Gray recalls his time there he still feels:

> The gales that from ye blow
> A momentary bliss bestow,
> As waving fresh their gladsome wing,
> My weary soul they seem to sooth.

But it is his 'weary soul' which is the Ode's dominant theme and the certitude of suffering.

> Alas, regardless of their doom,
> The little victims play!
> No sense have they of ills to come,
> Nor care beyond today:
> Yet see how all around 'em wait
> The Ministers of human fate,
> And black Misfortune's train!
> Ah, shew them where in ambush stand
> To seize their prey the murth'rous band!
> Ah, tell them, they are men!

The 'Ministers of human fate' which lie in wait in the following stanzas include Anger, Fear, Shame, Love, Jealousy, Envy, Care, Despair and Sorrow, a litany of horrors as Gray could have confidently expected his readers to recognise as being similar to those which gathered around Virgil at the entrance to the underworld in the 'Aeneid'. Leaving Eton and entering adulthood, he seems to be suggesting, is like entering the jaws of hell. We are beset, he says, by the 'Vultures of the Mind', and that his feelings about the fall-out with Walpole are still eating away at his mind are possibly being hinted at when he refers to:

> The stings of Falsehood those shall try
> And hard Unkindness' alter'd eye.

To the edition of 1768 he added an epigraph from Menander, 'I am a man and this is sufficient reason for being unhappy.' Yet from such despair he created a masterful poem which ends with lines of such compactness and precision that they have entered into the fabric of our language:

> And happiness too swiftly flies.
> Thought would destroy their paradise.
> No more; where ignorance is bliss,
> 'Tis folly to be wise.

And although often mis-quoted, another of Gray's lines which has become almost proverbial is, 'Nor all, that glisters, gold', the final line of his 'Ode on the Death of a Favourite Cat Drowned in a Tub of Goldfish'.

It had been sometime towards the end of February 1747 when Gray received a letter from Horace telling him of a domestic tragedy – that one of his cats had indeed fallen into a tub of goldfish and drowned. It is a pity we do not have this letter as it would be interesting to know what tone it was written in and how saddened Horace truly was. He had seemed to get over the death of his dog Tory very quickly after it had been carried off and eaten by a wolf. Gray, in his reply, seems uncertain how he ought to react. He was being asked to compose an elegy and he plays for time with a half-playful, half-formal hesitancy. Which cat, was it, he wants to know.

> As one ought to be particularly careful to avoid blunders in a compliment of condolence, it would be a sensible satisfaction to me (before I testify my sorrow, and the sincere part I take in your misfortune) to know for certain, who it is I lament. I knew Zara and Selima, (Selima, was it? or Fatima) or rather I knew them both together; for I cannot justly say which was which ... Till this affair is a little better determined, you will excuse me if I do not begin to cry: 'Tempus inane peto, requiem, spatiumque doloris.'

The ending being Dido's heartbroken cry! 'I beg for empty time, for peace, and reprieve from my frenzy.'

Selima, it proved to be, and a singularly appropriate name, being that of the heroine in Rowe's *Tamerlane*, for which Horace, as we have just seen, had written an Epilogue which was also included in Dodsley's anthology. By March 1st, in what can have been little more than a week, the poem was written and on its way to Walpole.

What never seems to have been questioned though is how exactly this tragic event came about. The *tub* is there to be seen today in Strawberry Hill and it really is not very big: in fact only 18 inches high and 21 inches across at the top (47 x 55cm). It must surely have been a tiny cat if it was unable to get out and drowned in such a small amount of water.

The poem itself is, as one would expect, an accomplished piece of work, a perfectly executed mock-heroic with, rather unexpectedly, great charm and wit.

> The hapless Nymph with wonder saw:
> A whisker first and then a claw,

> With many an ardent wish,
> She stretch'd in vain to reach the prize.
> What female heart can gold despise?
> What cat's averse to fish?

That second line so cleverly enacts and captures the slow, cautious approach and the thumping bathos of the last line is splendid. The sentiments might, of course, be accused of being a tad misogynistic, but then so is 'The Rape of the Lock' and who would want to be deprived of that most perfect of all poems?

While varying widely in their tone and topic, these three odes – 'On the Spring', 'A Distant prospect of Eton College' and 'The Death of a Favourite Cat' – have each a touch of mortality about them and this was soon to surface again in a poem so famous that it is always referred to simply as 'Gray's Elegy'. Samuel Johnson had little time or Gray: 'The poem on the Cat was doubtless considered by its author as a trifle, but it is not a happy trifle.' Yet even he was prepared to make an exception in the case of the 'Elegy', grumpily conceding that 'Had Gray written often thus, it had been vain to blame and useless to praise him.'

The 'Elegy' did not reach the public without a little touch of hysteria on Gray's part. He had sent a first draft of it to Horace, referring to it as 'a thing' he had written. Horace was naturally enthralled and began circulating copies of it among his friends, but without telling Gray. One copy unfortunately came into the hands of the editor of a decidedly downmarket periodical called *The Magazine of Magazines.* He contacted Gray to inform him that he intended to publish it, and naming him as the author, in the very next issue. Gray was, understandably, appalled. Horace had got him into this plight, so Horace had better get him out of it. His letter of 11th February 1751 begins abruptly, 'As you have brought me into a little Sort of Distress, you must assist me, I believe, to get out of it as well as I can' and after revealing the cause of this Distress, goes on, 'I have but one bad way left to escape the Honour they would inflict upon me & I am therefore obliged to desire you would make Dodsley print it immediately.' And the letter concludes, equally abruptly, 'If you behold the Mag. of Mag's in the Light that I do, you will not refuse to give yourself this Trouble on my Account, which you have taken of your own Accord before now. Adieu, Sir, I am Yours ever TG.' Gray was *on his dignity* again, but rightly so perhaps.

Happily the outcome was the publication and immediate acclaim of 'Elegy, wrote in a Country Church-yard' as he insisted 'the Title must be.' It was a happy outcome as otherwise it might have been difficult to persuade Gray to allow his poems to appear in print and if publication had been delayed until after his death, their effect would not have been the same.

The success of the 'Elegy' convinced Horace that a collection of Gray's poems should be published, even though his total output amounted to no more than six poems: the three which had already appeared in Dodsley's Anthology, plus the 'Elegy', the 'Long Story' and the 'Hymn to adversity'. But if Richard Bentley were to illustrate the poems, then it could prove to be a very attractive little volume. He put the proposal to Gray who immediately, and not unexpectedly, had qualms and objections. A book with only six poems in it would look ridiculous, but he had become an admirer of Bentley's work and so overcame his own scruples by insisting that his poems took second place, that, as he put it to Dodsley, they were 'only subordinate, and explanatory to the Drawings, and suffer'd by me to come out for that reason.' *suffer'd!* Another condition he imposed was that the book had to be called 'Designs by Mr R. Bentley for six poems by Mr T. Gray.' There is something patently absurd about it all, but they humoured him and Bentley began work on the illustrations in June 1751. By early 1753 the book was ready for publication, but at almost the last moment Gray discovered to his horror that Dodsley was planning to have a portrait of him by Eckhardt engraved as a frontispiece.

It was Walpole who was on the receiving end of Gray's outrage. 'Sure you are not out of your wits! This I know, if you suffer my Head to be printed, you infallibly will put me out of mine ... The Thing, I know, will make me ridiculous enough; but to appear in proper Person at the head of my works, consisting of half a dozen ballads in 30 pages, would be worse than the Pillory. I do assure you, if I had received such a book, with such a frontispiece without any warning, I believe it would have given me a Palsy.' When angry, he was not one to mince his words; it makes us realise that the falling-out in Reggio would not have been a gentlemanly, low-key affair.

When it appeared, even Gray must have accepted that it is a beautiful book. Printed, needless to say, without a frontispiece, but with a full-page illustration to each poem, often with an elaborate rococo border, an illustrated initial letter, together with a head-piece and a tail-piece.

Bentley's illustrations have come in for a variety of responses, varying from 'compelling originality and charm' to 'a barbaric and amateurish monstrosity', but it was left to Professor Loftus Jestin to show that they represent an important step in book illustration in that they are not simply pretty embellishments but develop, add to and complement the themes of the poems so that the odes and illustrations form a coherent whole. Professor

Jestin also asserts that the illustrations abound in puns, double entendres and 'pictorial improprieties'.

A close look at the full-page illustration for 'Ode on the death of a Favourite Cat' shows Selima precariously balanced on the rim of the tub while on either side are two Caryatids, one a river-god stopping his ears to her cries for help, the other Destiny cutting the nine (a nice touch) threads of her feline life. At the bottom are several mice clearly relishing the event. The initial letter shows her, 'demurest of the tabby kind', dozing in a chair while the head piece shows her drowning. But best of all is the tail-piece in which Charon is ferrying her over the River Styx and she is arching her back and spitting at the 'Hound of Hades', Cerberus.

Chief among the 'pictorial improprieties' to which Professor Jestin refers must surely be the skinny-dipping pupils depicted in the 'Prospect of Eton' ode, an illustration in which a bearded Old Father Thames, himself naked, is gazing down intently on their pert little bottoms protruding so provocatively from the 'glassy wave'. And there is more! How Walpole and Bentley, one suspects, must have chuckled over such an outrageous depiction of Gray's nostalgic and melancholy ode.

Having been so involved in the conception and design of the Bentley-Gray volume, Horace could now look upon himself as a publisher. The next logical step would be to consider establishing his own press, The Strawberry Hill Press.

6

THE STRAWBERRY-HILL PRESS

IN JULY 1757 HORACE WROTE TO Mann in Florence, 'I am turned printer, and have converted a little cottage here into a printing-office. My abbey is a perfect college or academy. I keep a painter [Müntz] in the house and a printer [Robinson] not to mention Mr Bentley who is an academy himself.' Typically, he did not want the project to be taken too seriously and mocked himself in a parody of a couplet by Pope.

> Some have at first for wits, then poets passed,
> Turned printers next, and proved plain fools at last.

It was the old dilemma: was this something a gentleman should do and what would people think of him? Would he look ridiculous? Would it look as though he had stooped to a trade? We can see from a remark made to William Mason that it was an issue which bothered him. 'I am neither ashamed of being an author, or a bookseller. My mother's father was a timber-merchant.'

Timothy Mowl, once again failing to understand Walpole, dismisses it as 'an eccentric venture of doubtful value.' Eccentric?

Yes, in that this was perhaps the first private printing press in the country, but one which was to become lastingly famous for producing beautiful books so valued that collectors and dealers bought them eagerly, and do so still. Again his standards were those of a professional. Mowl also accuses the press of being 'principally self-indulgence.' True, Horace published his own work, but fourteen books out of a total of thirty-four is not a disproportionate percentage and some of the others can be seen as acts of benevolence. In 1759 he published a small octavo, 'A Parallel in the Manner of Plutarch'. 700 copies were printed for the benefit of Mr Robert Hill, a poor tailor living in Buckingham, who 'in spite of overwhelming obstacles and abject poverty had become conversant in Latin, Greek and Hebrew.' Why Horace did this, we do not know, but, happily, we do know that 600 copies were sold in the first fortnight and all to the benefit of Mr Hill.

Printing was a trade, but it was not one from which Horace made any profit. A letter to Sir David Dalrymple in February 1764 gives a vivid account of the realities of the business.

> The London booksellers play me all manner of tricks. If I do not allow them ridiculous profit, they will do nothing to promote the sale; and when I do, they buy up the impression and sell it at an advanced price before my face ... In truth the plague I have had in every shape with my own printers, engravers, the booksellers, etc. bedside my own trouble have almost discouraged me from what I took up at first as an amusement, but which has produced very little of it. Or do our artists and booksellers cheat me because I am a gentleman? Whatever the cause, I am almost as sick of the profession of editor as of author. If I touch upon either more, it will be more idly, though chiefly because I never can be quite idle.

Gray had thought it was a silly scheme from the moment he first heard of it, telling his friend James Brown, ' ... you must know (what you will like no more than I do, yet it were not in my power anyhow to avoid it) that Mr W has set up a printing-press in his own house in Twickenham.' When Horace sent him some works from the press, he was not enthusiastic, beginning rather patronisingly, 'They are very pleasant to the eye and will do no dishonour to your press.' Then adding, 'As you are but young in your trade, you will excuse me if I tell you that some little inaccuracies have escaped your eye.' There followed a list of misplaced apostrophes (in plural nouns no less!) missing capital letters and commas where they shouldn't be and not where they should. Horace accepted the criticisms, adding, so very tellingly, 'And I hope future edition mongers will say of those of Strawberry Hill, they have all the beautiful negligence of a gentleman.'

Nevertheless, Gray had by that time already agreed to the Strawberry Hill Press publishing his two Pindaric odes, 'The Progress of Poetry' and 'The Bard'. Horace had made the announcement in a letter to Mann in August 1757:

> I send you two copies of a very honourable opening of my press – two amazing Odes of Mr Gray; they are Greek, they are Pindaric, they are sublime! consequently, I fear, a little obscure ... I could not persuade him to add more notes; he says whatever wants to be explained, don't deserve to be.

It was indeed a very honourable opening to his press. A thousand copies were printed – more than any later volume – and sold by Dodsley they earned Gray the sum of £40.

Horace always had a whimsical sense of humour and in the

early days of the Press when Lady Townsend and two of her companions were being shown around the house, he had primed the press in advance so that, as if by magic, it suddenly printed off a poem addressed to her personally.

The press speaks:

> From me wits and poets their glory obtain;
> Without me their wits and their verses were vain.
> Stop, Townsend, and let me but paint what you say;
> You, the fame I on others bestow, will repay.

Small wonder that he was so popular with ladies. The verse might have won him no bays as a poet, but such gallantry and charm delighted them.

After the publication of Gray's Odes the next book to come off the Press was Walpole's own *A Catalogue of Royal and Noble Authors,* which is just what the title says it is. Peter Sabor, the recent editor of Walpole's *'Works'* saw it as 'a futile undertaking' and declared that 'there is something perverse about the whole enterprise.' On the face of it that would seem hard to argue with, yet the facts do not bear this out. Horace printed three hundred copies which went chiefly to his antiquarian friends and their reception encouraged him to sell the copyright to Dodsley for £200, which instantly and generously went to Bentley to allow him to return from his debtors' retreat in Jersey. Dodsley was confident enough to print two thousand copies. Six further editions came out in Horace's lifetime and several more in the nineteenth century. Rather than *futile* it seems to have had a solid reputation as a valuable reference book. The *Gentleman's Magazine,* while for the most part critical, recognised the 'diligence and labour' which had gone into it and it is true that Horace's friends in Florence and Rome had scoured the libraries there for him. Much like Gray, but with a more positive outcome, Horace himself clearly delighted in such research.

Edmund Burke in a review in the *Annual Register* has it right when he observes, 'Very few writers, however, could have had the happy secret of making out of so dry a matter so agreeable an entertainment and of uniting so much laborious industry in the compiling with so much wit and spirit in the execution.' What Horace has done is to combine perfectly the two sides of his nature. As Owen Ruffhead wrote in the *Monthly Review* of December 1758, 'The Author has happily blended the gentleman with the scholar.' His thoroughgoing scholarship has enabled him to write something a gentleman may read with pleasure. As he put it himself, rather coyly ' ... this is intended as a treatise of curiosity, calculated for the closets of the idle and inquisitive.'

And so, if we happen to have some idle moments and feel sufficiently inquisitive, let us retire to our closets with it, but always remembering the closing lines of Horace's Introduction, 'This work was calculated to amuse: if it offends any man, or is taken too seriously, the author will be concerned; but it will never make him so serious as to defend it.'

It begins with the Royal Authors, starting with Richard I and one's first impression is that it is not at all amusing, even in an 18th century sense of the word. It is exactly what it says – a catalogue of those writings which can be positively shown to have been written by them. Some entries are astonishing: that Queen Elizabeth translated into Latin two orations of Socrates and a play by Euripides. But among the introductory asides there is enough to encourage further dipping. Edward VI, we are told, wrote a comedy called 'The Whore of Babylon'. Horace lets fly, 'What an education for a great prince, to be taught to scribble controversial ribaldry! As elegant as it is said to have been, I question whether it surpassed the other buffooneries which engrossed the theatres of Europe in that and the preceding century.'

When we turn from the Royal to the Noble Authors the very first sentence is promising: 'The abolition of taste and literature were not the slightest abuses proceeding from popery.' The catalogue element is now less prominent, the introductions longer, vigorous and assertive. 'In those rude ages when valour and ignorance were the attributes of nobility...' This is the opening of some paragraphs on John Tiptoft, Earl of Worcester who has fallen into total obscurity, as is true of the majority of the entries. And when we do come to names we know, the literary content can be disappointing. Henry Howard, Earl of Surrey, is known today for having introduced the Shakespearian sonnet form and for the first use of blank verse in his translation of Virgil, two very notable achievements, and yet all Horace tells us is, 'We have a small volume of elegant and tender sonnets composed by Surrey and with them some others of that age, particularly of Sir Thomas Wyatt, the elder, a very accomplished gentleman.' And yet these gentlemen were, one might say, the founding fathers of English poetry. But Sir Philip Sidney comes in for a drubbing. Horace cannot understand why he is so highly rated. 'What do we find?' he asks, and answers his own question – ' ... a tedious, lamentable, pedantic, pastoral romance, which the patience of a young virgin in love cannot now wade through; and some absurd attempts to fetter English verse to Roman chains.' Later in the book, under Peeresses, the Countess of Pembroke is also given short shrift, brushed aside as 'The celebrated sister of Sir Philip Sidney.'

Lord Herbert of Cherbury is included, 'One of the greatest ornaments of the learned peerage', but not his brother George because he had no title. This is the oddity of the enterprise, a work on English authors without any mention of Spenser, Shakespeare, Jonson ... It would seem that Horace had little interest in what his authors wrote. He roundly attacks Antony Ashley Cowper, Earl of Shaftsbury, who 'canted tyranny under Cromwell, practised it under Charles', but fails to mention Dryden's assassination of him in 'Absalom and Achitophel' which is too good not to be quoted here.

> Of these the false Achitophel was first:
> A name to all succeeding Ages curst.
> For close Designs, and crooked Counsels fit;
> Restless, unfixt in Principles and Place;
> In Power unpleas'd, impatient of Disgrace.
> A fiery Soul, which working out its way
> Fretted the Pigmy Body to decay.

Apart from Gray, Horace seems to have little time for poets. 'I can't bear modern poetry,' he had told Mann, and when his own poetry was praised he insisted 'I never thought poetry excusable' and that to be called a poet made him 'as silly a fellow as [James] Thomson.' In the briefest of references to the development of prose style, we find to our surprise that his highest praise is reserved for his tutor, Conyers Middleton, by whom it was raised to 'classic elegance and force.' Hardly an unbiased evaluation and one rather hard to credit.

People were what really interested him, and scattered through these pages are some wonderful sketches. George Villiers, Duke of Buckingham being one:

> When this extraordinary man, with the figure and genius of Alcibiades, could equally charm the Presbyterian Fairfax, and the dissolute Charles; when he alike ridiculed that witty king and his solemn chancellor; when he plotted the ruin of his country with a cabal of bad ministers, or equally unprincipled supported its cause with bad patriots; one laments that such parts should have been devoid of every virtue.

Sir Francis Bacon is passed over very briefly, however, on the grounds that his life story was already too well known to need repeating and this does lend support to Macaulay's extravagant objection that:

> He rejects all but the attractive parts of his subject. He keeps only what is in itself amusing, or what can be made so by the artifice of his diction. The coarser morsels of antiquarian learning he abandons to others; and sets out an entertainment worthy of a Roman epicure – an entertainment consisting of nothing but delicacies – the brains of singing birds, the roe of mullets, the sunny halves of peaches.

But this had always been Horace's intention – to entertain. Even the recherché epigraph from Cardinal D'Este to Ariosto, on his title page had been self-deprecating 'Dove, diavalo! Messer Ludovicio, avete pigliato tante coglionerie?' (Where the Devil, Sir Ludovicio, did you collect so many imbecilities?)

Yet there is also, at the same time, something approaching a sub-text and that is the work's political content. Viewed as a whole, it could be looked upon as the expression of a debt of gratitude to this father, to whom he so often pays tribute. At the end of his account of Edward Montagu, Earl of Sandwich, he cannot resist pointing out that 'It is remarkable that admiral Montagu was the last commoner who was honoured with the garter, except one man, to whose virtues and merit may some impartial pen do as much justice as I have satisfaction in rendering to this great person!' The exception having being Sir Robert, and in the closing stages of the book, two pages are given to defending him passionately against the charge of what seems like a very small demeanour. But the clearest sign of Horace's devotion to the memory of his father is the steadfastness with which he adheres to his Whig principles of liberty against Tory insistence on the royal prerogative.

As by definition all the authors in this catalogue were wealthy and powerful, it is inevitable that they were also involved in politics and as he relates incidents from their lives, anecdotal though they often are, the struggle between the liberty of the people and the authority of the crown is highlighted again and again. At the root of Horace's political ideal was *balance*, such as was achieved by his father and by which he maintained that equilibrium between Parliament and the monarchy, which ensured twenty years of stability. Throughout Horace defends 'those heroes who withstood the arbitrary proceedings of Charles I and his ministers and to whose spirit we owe so much of our liberty.'

His defence of the regicides could not be more forceful: 'If a king deserves to be opposed by force of arms, he deserves death; if he reduces his subjects to that extremity, the blood spilt in the quarrel lies on him ... the executing him afterwards is a mere formality.' The word *mere* comes with such a shock.

And again, in his account of Edward Hyde, Earl of Clarendon, he re-states his position: 'Like Justice itself, he held the balance between the necessary power of the supreme magistrate and the interests of the people. This never-dying obligation his contemporaries were taught to overlook and to clamour against, till they removed the only man who, if he could, would have corrected his master's evil government.'

Just how far Horace's republicanism went it is hard to tell. In a footnote to his entry on Edward Montagu we find, 'It is supposed that no country is so *naturally* propense to *liberty* as England – Is it *naturally* propense to *Monarchy*? Is *Monarchy* the natural vehicle of liberty?'

But when a Republic was established in France, he was equally forceful. The final sentence in the Appendix to the *Catalogue* reads:

> N.B. This addition was written before the Revolution in France in 1789; since when the follies of that nation have soured and plunged into the most execrable barbarity, immorality, injustice, usurpation and tyranny; have rejected God himself and deified human monsters and have dared to call this mass of unheard of crimes 'giving liberty to mankind' – by atheism and massacres!

His outrage in this instance is understandable and he was perfectly right in seeing it as a new form of tyranny, and when there was even the possibility of such a thing coming close to home, he was far from happy about it. In 1765, the weavers of London were suffering a catastrophic fall in trade due to cheap imports and they petitioned Parliament for some assistance. The

Commons was in favour, but the Lords threw out the idea, so the weavers besieged Parliament and attacked Lord Bedford's house, seeing him as largely responsible for it. Horace had supported the Bill, but an attack on a Lord's house was quite another matter. Then there were rumours of weavers from Norfolk and Manchester marching towards London and even of sailors from Portsmouth joining them. This was going too far. 'There is such a general spirit of mutiny and dissatisfaction in the lower people, that I think we are in danger of rebellion in the heart of the capital,' he wrote to Lord Hertford. The use of military force – 'several regiments' – met with his approval and the turmoil caused by these 'lower people' was put down; a cavalry charge being used to disperse one gathering.

Horace seems to have been, in many ways, a theoretical liberal, but in many other practical ways he was an aristocratic liberal. When his insane nephew died in 1791 and he became Lord Orford, he expressed his happiness that the death 'has restored me to my birthright'.

A *Catalogue of the Royal and Noble Authors of England* was what the book had innocently set out to be, but allowing it to become interlaced with so many of his own personal views and prejudices, and often in such a casual and anecdotal way, was what gave it its special appeal, but also what brought him into trouble. Someone was bound to be offended. As the *Gentleman's Magazine* observed, 'There are, in some passages, traces of party zeal, and there are some which seem to favour more natural religion as distinct from Christianity.' Politics and religion – a fatal mixture, and indeed complaints and criticisms, some even in pompous pamphlet form, came flooding in. This was not what

Horace had expected. As he wrote with charming honesty to a new friend, Dr Henry Zouch, 'Few men are capable of forgiving being told their faults in private – who can bear being told of them publicly?' He certainly could not, adding, 'I am sick of the character of author, I am sick of the consequences of it. I am weary of seeing my own name in the newspapers, I am tired with reading foolish criticisms on me, and as foolish defences of me.'

But he does not seem to have been as sick of it as he claimed, for later in 1758 he published 200 copies of *Fugitive Pieces in Verse and Prose,* a collection of some earlier poems and prose pieces he had contributed to *The Museum* and *The World.* The following year, however, things began to go badly wrong. When he had engaged William Robinson as his first printer he thought he had, 'The most sensible look in the world.' Eventually he proved to be 'a foolish Irishman who took himself to be a genius' and when Horace told him that he was 'extremely the former and not the least of the latter' he took umbrage and decamped. He was succeeded by Benjamin Williams who stayed less than two months, then came James Lister who left after a week. Two others, Farmer and Pratt came and went and the press ceased altogether. Worse, the painter, John Henry Müntz left. 'The substance was extreme impertinence to me,' he told Montagu, 'and I was forced to turn him out of doors.' Worse still, the idleness and extravagance of Richard Bentley, once regarded as 'an academy in himself', had now tried Horace's patience long enough, and he too was shown the door.

One change led to another, and he turned his attention to the building. As far back as September 1758 he had written to Mann, 'A day may come that will produce a gallery, a round tower, a large cloister, and a cabinet in the manner of a little chapel.' And now that day had come. Work began in 1760 and one of the consequences was the pulling down of the old Printing House and the erection of a new, purpose-built one which to judge from a contemporary illustration was high-ceilinged, spacious and well-lit, as one would expect seeing that it was to house one of the most distinguished private presses of all time. Unfortunately, an opportunity was later missed which would have made Strawberry Hill books even more collectable. John Baskerville, whose typeface is still so renowned, sent Horace a few specimens of his work and enquired as to some possible support. At that time his business was not going well; indeed it was a business, he said, 'which I am heartily tired of, and wish I had never attempted.' Horace's reply is not recorded, but the golden partnership never took place. At the same time that all this new building was progressing, so Horace was turning over in his mind ideas for a new book.

***

One of the most accomplished antiquaries and engravers in England in the eighteenth century was George Vertue. Trained under Sir Godfrey Kneller, he was appointed engraver to the Society of Antiquaries in 1717 at the age of 33, and enjoyed the patronage of Robert Harley, Earl of Oxford, the Duke of Norfolk and even the Prince of Wales. Travelling with such men gave him a first-hand knowledge of all the finest art collections in the country, including that of Horace's father at Houghton.

Wherever he went, he kept copious records of all he saw, intending to publish a *History of the Arts in England*, but when he died in 1756 he had not even begun work on it. He left behind over 40 years of notes, sketches, jottings and essays in 40 small notebooks which Horace bought from his widow in 1758 for £100. These notebooks became the foundation of his own scholarly and monumental work, *Anecdotes of Painting in England*.

Whether Horace had had an opportunity to look closely at these little notebooks before he bought them we do not know, but when he did he must surely have flinched at the enormity of the task ahead of him. Firstly, some of Virtue's handwriting was so small he needed a magnifying glass to read it at all. What's more, there was no organisation to the notebooks; they were, he said, 'a heap of immethodic confusion' with separate references to any particular painter scattered about in several volumes. The solution he decided on was not that of a dilettante. What he needed, he could see, was an index. Without one he could never find his way through the maze of information. Now only those who have ever constructed an index by hand can appreciate the long hours of mind-deadening labour it involves, so we are full of admiration and then left speechless when we read in a letter to George Montagu of 1770, 'I have lost my index and am forced again to turn over all 40 volumes of miniature MSS, so this will be the third time I shall have made an index. Don't say I am not persevering.'

No, no one could accuse him of that, nor question his industry. In his *Catalogue of Engravers* he said of Robert White, 'As my author had formed a long list, it would be defrauding curious collectors if I refused to transcribe it; one would not grudge a few hours more, after the many that have been thrown away on these idle volumes.'

He began writing in January 1760, had finished the first volume by August, and the second by October, assisted in this, as he confessed, by a severe attack of gout which kept him from doing very little else. Nevertheless it was a task which did require all his industry as he was not simply copying and editing; he was collating and re-writing, checking sources, making corrections, adding his own discoveries and doing so in his own lively and polished style. It proved to be a masterly and pioneering work as George Vertue was not his only source. There was his own knowledge and expertise. He had catalogued his father's collection at Houghton and between 1751 and 1784 it has been calculated by Paget Toynbee that he visited 45 country estates and studied their collections. Added to which he had his own vast collection of prints and miniatures.

It is difficult to know how Horace intended his readers to approach the work. Had he meant it to be *read*, he would surely have ensured that the opening pages were more interesting, whereas he makes it evident that throughout the fourteenth century there was little to record or which was worth recording. He refers to the *Anecdotes* as 'designed for a work of curiosity', suggesting a work of reference, something to be consulted. Nevertheless, as he said in a 1762 letter to the Rev Henry Zouch, 'I do not see why books of antiquities should not be made as amusing as writing on any other subject.' Equally we must guard against being misled by the word *Anecdotes* in the title. In the eighteenth century it did not mean chit-chat; Johnson defines it as 'hitherto unpublished narratives or details of history.' The work does indeed fulfil both criteria. It is a work of scholarship which, if dipped into, will be found to be readable and entertaining.

Acknowledging how much is owed to a rival or a predecessor is a debt which authors are not always eager to repay. The Rev Thomas Percy, for instance, took full credit for what is always known as *Percy's Reliques of English Poetry*, even though it was William Shenstone, recently and conveniently deceased, who had done almost all the editorial work, but received no more that a cursory nod in passing. In contrast, Horace was warmly generous in his account of George Virtue, praising his 'indefatigable pains' and saying that, 'he left nothing unexplored that could illuminate his subject', yet not attempting to cover up 'the indigested method of his collection.'

In the opening pages of his Preface, Horace reminds his readers that England, unlike Italy and France, did not possess a history of its painters, while admitting that, 'the country has very rarely given birth to a genius in that profession.' But his hope was that this was about to change, that there were signs that the arts and sciences were beginning to flourish in an increasingly prosperous society. A passionate believer in liberty, he accepts that 'a good government, that indulges its subjects in the exercise of their own thoughts, will see a thousand inventions spring up and refinements will follow.' By a good government he meant, it hardly needs saying, a Whig government. Politics was never far from his mind and he goes further, 'Arts that are innocent in themselves and beneficial to the country, either by adding value to our productions, or by drawing riches as they invite strangers to visit us, are worthy of the attention of good citizens; and in all those lights that society acts upon a national and extensive plan.' And he was not only perceptive, he was right. England was about to witness an age of great painters and the building of great houses.

The Preface concludes on a note of modesty, 'They who cannot perform great things themselves, may have the satisfaction of doing justice to those who can.' He soon had the satisfaction of reading some very positive reviews. An anonymous writer in the *Critical* declared that 'from a long acquaintance with, and attachment to the polite arts, [Mr Walpole] has so formed his judgement, and improved his taste, as to be looked up to by the *cognoscenti* as a judge and dictator in every thing that concerns them.' But most pleasing of all must have been a letter he received from an accomplished antiquarian, the Rev William Cole. He declared that the work was 'a continual feast from one end to the other', but went on to add that, 'I met with two or three errata, or false printings, which I hope you will excuse me from pointing out.' The tact is magnificent as what followed was page after page of corrections or 'trifling observations' as he called them. Instead of being put out by it all, Horace, to his great credit, was so pleased that it was the start of a close friendship and a twenty year exchange of letters.

The information in the opening chapters is of little interest – the 14th century being a time of war and conflict and so hardly conducive to the creation of works of art – yet Horace's asides can be perceptive. The rulers were, he reminds us, ' ... proud, warlike and ignorant nobility and encouraged only that brand [of the arts] which attested their dignity or served to display their wealth.' His own wry sense of humour is evident when he tells us that Henry VII was happy to be lavish in the design of his own tomb, 'comforted by the thought that it would not be paid for until after his death.'

As the work progresses and we move into more recent times,

so these nuggets expand, and though most of the names, it has to be said, mean nothing to us now, one cannot help but be impressed by the research that has gone into it. Equally impressive and delightful are the engravings of the artists themselves; the beards and moustachios alone are a constant delight, particularly those of the eponymous Henry Cornelius Vroom.

Even when considering works of art, politics were never far from Horace's mind. He was prepared to credit Charles I with being the first monarch 'of real taste in England' and to praise him for 'the rewards he bestowed on men of true genius and merit', but could not resist adding, 'Charles had virtues to make a nation happy; fortunate, if he had not thought that he alone knew how to make them happy, and that he alone ought to have the power of making them so!' But he could be even-handed. The puritans' destruction of religious paintings the moment Charles was dead is castigated as 'a piece of fanatic bigotry that was perfectly ridiculous.'

In the pages which follow are several extended essays, perceptive and informed, on, among others, Rubens, Van Dyke, Inigo Jones and Grinling Gibbons. In them he could be warmly appreciative, observing how Gibbons, 'gave to wood the loose and airy lightness of flowers, and chained together the various productions of the elements with a free disorder natural to each species'. Equally, he could be critical, adding as a footnote to a comment on Van Dyke's draperies, 'His satins, of which he was fond, particularly white and blue, are remarkably finished; his back grounds heavy, and have great sameness.' Throughout there is an assuredness, such that in 1931 an article in the TLS was still able to assert that, 'Scholars have long treated

'Anecdotes on Painting' as the ultimate authority on the subject of English arts.'

It is not only on the subject of painting that his expertise is evident. As one would expect, his views on architecture feature some of his most vigorous writing, especially where the Gothic is concerned: 'This Saxon (by which he means Norman) style begins to be defined by flat and round arches ... and by a very few other characteristics, all evidence of barbarous and ignorant times ... Beautiful Gothic architecture was grafted on Saxon deformity.' Grecian architecture fares no better: 'It is difficult for the noblest Grecian temple to convey half so many impressions to the mind as a cathedral does of the best Gothic taste.' And one of his most famous assertions, 'One must have taste to be sensible of the beauties of Grecian architecture; one only wants passions to feel Gothic.'

Coming nearer to his own time he is totally contemptuous of Sir John Vanbrugh, 'He undertook vast designs and composed heaps of littleness ... He seems to have hollowed quarries rather than to have built houses.' The architect of Strawberry Hill could hardly be expected to have much sympathy with the likes of Blenheim and Castle Howard, ' ... ponderous and unmeaning masses which overwhelmed architecture into mere masonry.' The very sound of that sentence itself seems to mimic their structure.

The most celebrated of his essays comes in Volume IV in which he celebrates William Hogarth. It is an essay which begins so delightfully: 'Having dispatched the herd of our painters in oil, I reserve to a class by himself that great and original genius, Hogarth.' His initial approach to Hogarth is so perceptive and so very much his own. Catching the manners and follies of an age is, he says, *comedy* and he therefore compares Hogarth's satires with the dramatists, Congreve and Molière, pointing out that there is intrigue being carried on throughout in his *Marriage à-la-mode*.

> Thus there is wit in the figure of the alderman, who, when his daughter is expiring in the agonies of poison, wears a face of solicitude – but it is to save her gold ring which he is drawing gently from her finger. The thought is parallel to Molière's, where the miser puts out one of the candles as he is talking.'

It is clear that Hogarth meets with deepest approval when he asserts that 'amidst all his pleasantry he observes the true end of comedy, reformation; there is always a moral to his pictures', but adding, to his honour, that 'ill-nature did not guide his pencil' nor did he 'condescend to explain his moral lessons by the trite poverty of allegory.' It is there in the detail, he tells us, such detail as a spider's web covering the poor-box in a parish church.

> Mirth coloured his pictures, but benevolence designed them. He smiled like Socrates, that men might not be offended at his lectures, and might learn to laugh at their own follies.

However, having extolled his satires, he bluntly states that:

> ... as a painter [of history] he had but slender merit ... not only his colouring and drawing rendered him unequal to the task, the genius that had entered so feelingly into the calamities and crimes of familiar life, deserted him in a walk that called for dignity and grace.

There are sometimes views, as here, that one might wish to

challenge, but they are delivered with sensitivity and vigour and one might wish that more art criticism were written so.

It was the 'Advertisement to the Fourth Volume', however, written in 1768 which occasioned more comment and controversy than anything else in all the other volumes. In it he says he would rather leave it to posterity to treat of the living, but then suggests what the findings of posterity might be. After a quick glance at 'the taste and vigour' of the architecture of Burlington and Kent, he passes on to painting, claiming that there is no one in Italy 'to rival an imagination so fertile as that of Sir Joshua Reynolds' or the 'frankness of nature in Mr Gainsborough's landscapes'. And that, seemingly, is felt to be quite enough. But when he turns to three contemporary women artists, he praises them at extravagant length, particularly Lady Diana Beauclerk. He cannot praise her enough. After citing her 'singular genius and taste', he says, 'these imperfect encomiums are far short of the excellence of her works.'

At least this shows that Horace was no prude. She had been married earlier to the Second Viscount Bolingbroke and their divorce had been one of the most prolonged and scandalous of the century. When she married Topham Beauclerk two days after the divorce in 1773, Johnson rebuffed Boswell's attempts to side with her, 'The woman's a whore, Sir, and there's an end on't.' Curiously, her maiden name had been Lady Diana Spenser.

Three years later Horace wrote to tell Lady Ossory that he had added to Strawberry Hill 'one of those tall thin Flemish towers that are crowned with a sort of extinguisher.' He called it *The Beauclerk Tower* as he had had it built specifically to display 'the incomparable drawings' she had made of his Gothic play, *The Mysterious Mother*. It was a tiny tower, no more than 9' in diameter and only the closest of his friends were ever allowed access to it. The value he put on these drawings is evident from a letter he wrote to Horace Mann: 'Lady Diana Beauclerk has drawn 7 scenes from *The Mysterious Mother* – such drawings. Salvator Rossa and Guido could not surpass their expression and beauty.' Yet in her *Anecdotes of Walpole*, Lady Laetitia-Matilda Hawkins declared that, 'they can be looked upon only with disgust and contempt.' This is going perhaps too far as now that we have the opportunity to view them online they look far from remarkable, indeed innocuous rather than exotic. The characters she depicts are static; there are no bodies inside the clothes they wear. The faces of the women all look very alike and have absurdly melodramatic expressions. One of the oddest features is that in every picture a good deal of space is taken up by the floppy branches of what might be a weeping cypress tree, but which is very badly drawn.

Mr Ketton-Cremer, Walpole's most sympathetic biographer, said that, 'These outbursts of facile enthusiasm have done great damage to his reputation as a critic, alike in the eyes of his contemporaries and of posterity.' Horace was not totally alone in his estimation, however, Reynolds praised her and Wedgwood used several of her designs. But even W.H. Lewis's attempt to defend him falls somewhat short: 'The discovery of talent in persons of quality whose gifts were generally unrecognised gave Walpole, champion of the neglected, great pleasure.'

Lewis's term 'unrecognised' is certainly not one which could be applied to the sculptress Anne Damer, regarded by Horace as a second Praxiteles. Her family connections to the Walpoles make it look initially like special pleading. She was the only child of the

Conways, so Horace was not only her uncle, he had also been her godfather and she had frequently stayed at Strawberry Hill when she was a child. 'I love her as my own child,' he once declared to Horace Mann. But this being said, she was no amateur. She was an honorary member of the Royal Academy and 32 of her works had been displayed there.

Curiously, she was even more notorious than Lady Beauclerk. Married at 17 to John Damer, the reprobate son of Lord Milton, she left him after 7 years, by which time he had run up debts of £70,000, debts which his father refused to meet. As Horace recounts in a letter to Mann, Damer went to the Bedford Arms in Soho one evening in August 1776 having pre-ordered a dinner there. With him went four prostitutes and a blind fiddler and when the evening's 'entertainment' drew to a close he sat down in an armchair and shot himself. Luckily, Mrs Damer had a pre-nuptial agreement whereby her father-in-law was obliged to pay her £2,500 a year, which enabled her to travel widely – she was even granted an audience with Napoleon – and to train professionally as a sculptor. Among her creations were busts of Fox, Nelson, Sir Joseph Banks, and George III. Sculpture had always been seen as a man's world and she came in for some hostility, especially as she made no effort to hide her 'sapphism', as it was then called. Her fame, or notoriety, can be seen from the fact that she featured in satirical cartoons. In one by William Holland in 1789 she is seen carving a male nude and what she is doing to his bottom with her chisel looks less than artistic. In contrast, Sir Joshua Reynolds had painted a fine portrait of her the year before. It is evident that Horace's view of her work was widely shared. Sir William Hamilton declared of one of her works, 'in my opinion there is not an artist now in Italy that could have done it with so much of the true sublime.' And that she inherited a lifetime tenancy of Strawberry Hill when Horace died must be proof of her personal worth. Nevertheless it is hard to equate the extended praise given to these ladies with the perfunctory nods bestowed on Reynolds and Gainsborough, especially considering that Reynolds had not only painted Walpole, but also the *Committee of Taste*.

Volumes I and II of the 'Anecdotes of Painting in England' appeared as a small quarto edition of 600 copies in 1762, Volume III in 1763 and Volume IV in 1780. The printer responsible for the final edition was one Thomas Kirkgate, whose arrival in 1765 was a blessing after the succession of eccentrics and incompetents who had passed through earlier. As well as being highly skilled in his trade, Kirkgate was also a man of some education and culture who stayed with Horace right to the end, acting as his secretary and amanuensis when writing proved too painful for him, even managing to imitate his handwriting so well that collectors have sometimes been deceived. Yet after a quarter of a century of loyal service, Horace left him only £100 in his will, at which he was not best pleased, as can be seen from a poem 'The Printer's Farewell to Strawberry Hill', written on his behalf by the miniaturist Septimus Harding.

> Adieu! Ye Groves and Gothic Tow'rs,
> Where I have spent my youthful Hours,
>   Alas! I find in vain:
> Since he who could my age protect,
> By some mysterious, sad neglect,
>   Has left me to complain!

> For thirty years of Labour past
> To meet such slight Regard at last
>   Has added to my Cares:
> To quit the quiet Scenes of Life
> T'encounter Bus'ness, Bustle Strife,
>   Hangs heavy on my Years.
>
> Farewell! my Printing House, farewell!
> Where I no more shall calmly dwell,
>   Within thy peaceful Door;
> No more in Conversation free,
> Enjoy my Friend, and sip my Tea;
>   Ah! no, those Days are o'er.
>
> On thee my Fellow-Lab'rour dear,
> My Press, I drop the silent Tear
>   Of Pity for thy Lot;
> For thee, like me, by Time art worn,
> Like me, too, thou art left forlorn,
>   Neglected and forgot!

That a *Friend* should have treated him so badly is surprising, but there is another side to the issue. When he died, the auction of his possessions went on for ten days, realised over £800 and included the first offer of a complete set, plus duplicates, of all Strawberry Hill's editions. Kirkgate had evidently been printing – even re-printing the earliest editions – for himself and in all probability selling privately during his lifetime. Horace, no fool, would seem to have been aware of this, and was letting him know from beyond the grave.

What he would not have known is that Kirkgate had made copies of certain passages in the correspondence to Mann, passages which he knew were to be suppressed and he seemingly attempted to blackmail the executors; his daughter ultimately surrendering them to Mrs Damer in whose presence they were destroyed. Mrs Damer, who had inherited Strawberry Hill, lost no time in turning the Printing House into a studio for her own sculpture, and so ended the Press.

7

THE GARDEN

In his 'Epistle to Lord Burlington', Alexander Pope delivers his directives on landscape gardening, one of the most memorable being 'In all, let Nature never be forgot.' But what a slippery and elusive word *Nature* has proved to be, applying itself to totally dissimilar aesthetic ideals. Twenty years previously, in his 'Essay on Criticism' he had written:

> Learn hence from ancient Rules a just Esteem,
> To copy Nature is to copy them.

To do so would have been to accept the classical ideals of orderliness, symmetry and proportion, ideals which we see linked in Pope's own adherence to the heroic couplet, the architecture of Christopher Wren and the great formal gardens such as those at Fontainebleau. There the Grand Canal runs straight as an arrow for at least a mile, and the perfect square of the ornamental lake is edged with gravel walks, edged in their turn by identical, well-disciplined trees. But what is special about Fontainebleau is that another of its features is *un jardin anglais* where there are no straight lines, where narrow paths backed by irregular clusters of shrubs and trees go randomly wandering about in a grassy valley and where there are flowers and a little stream meanders under a 'rustic' bridge.

Nowhere else shows so clearly, and in such proximity, the contrast between the two notions of what constitutes a garden. The Frenchman, Le Nôtre, architect of Versailles, is said to have regarded a piece of land as a bare space on which a design might be created. We can have no notion now of what the formal gardens at Fontainebleau had *previously* been like. In contrast, in the *English Garden*, Nature has not been forgotten. The individuality of the locale has been recognised. It may have been *composed*, enhanced by a little *art*, but it has not had a hard discipline imposed upon it. The designer had, in Pope's words, consulted 'the Genius of the Place.' It was its *inherent beauty* which had been developed.

The culture, both social and intellectual, behind such disparate concepts and how in England the one so quickly gave way to the other is accounted for in what is unquestionably the most succinct and informed garden history of its day: Horace Walpole's 'On Modern Gardening'. In 1802 Sir Humphrey Repton wrote, 'I scarcely need mention the late Horace Walpole, who in his lively and ingenious manner, has given both the history and the rules of the art better than any other theorist.'

Published in 1780 it comes at the end of the fourth volume of his 'Anecdotes of Painting in England', which is not really surprising as for Horace there always had been a clear link between paintings and landscapes. Having for so long been engaged in buying, arranging and hanging pictures, he tended to look at nature through eyes accustomed to seeing it as depicted by painters such as Rossa and Poussin for whom landscape was no longer simply a background against which to portray some human activity, but a subject in its own right. Sir Robert had no less than nine of their original works on his walls at Houghton.

Painters were not alone in adopting a new approach; philosophers too were finding a new beauty in Nature. In 1713 in his 'Characteristics' Shaftesbury had written:

> The rude rocks, the mossy caverns, the irregular unwrought grottos and broken falls of water, with all the horrid graces of the wilderness itself, as representing Nature more, will be the more engaging and appear with a magnificence beyond the formal mockery of Princely Gardens.

As Burke was to develop in his 'Philosophical Enquiry into the Origen of Our Ideas of the Sublime and the Beautiful' in 1757, it was an appreciation of Nature for its own sake: no moral implications, but a recognition that such scenes might call up memories and evoke feelings of pleasure and of the sublime. As in pictures, so in gardens. A ruin might suggest, as Shenstone put it, 'that pleasing melancholy which proceeds from a reflexion on decayed magnificence'; a hermitage or a Greek temple offer a sense of the divine, while the paintings might long afterwards remind the owners of their youthful travels abroad. A feeling for natural beauty was now seen as a genuine aesthetic experience.

It could be argued that it was the Grand Tour which largely accounted for these changes, as a new generation, brought up on the Classics, encountered the actuality of the Italian landscape and saw for the first time the Alps and its rugged and irregular pastoral scenery. Returning home, they brought back not only their memories but countless copies of Rossa and Poussin. Many also learned to sketch and paint for themselves and so became actively engaged in the landscape. Even Alexander Pope had taken painting lessons from Charles Jervas and is recorded as having declared that, 'all gardening is landscape painting.'

As early as 1739, when only in his twenties, we can see that Horace's response to what he saw was equally picture-based. Writing to his school friend Richard West, about the Alps and the Grand Chartreuse, he said, 'Did you ever see anything like the prospect we saw yesterday. I never did!' A *Prospect,* is defined by Johnson as, 'A picturesque representation of landscape.' And Horace concludes, 'We stopped there two hours, rode back through the charming picture, wished for a painter – wished we were poets!' For Horace it was all surface – all in the eye. There is no sense whatsoever of the sublime. Whereas, alongside him was a poet and Gray's response was strikingly different. In his letter – also to West – he claims the scene was, 'pregnant with religion and poetry,' adding 'scenes that would awe an atheist into belief.' Their characters and attitudes had evidently developed early.

Opposed as he was to the artificiality of the French style, Horace nevertheless saw the creation of a garden as an *art*. The Art of the Picturesque. Prefacing his chapter on *Paintings in the Reign of George II* he admits that the English had produced few painters of note, but asserts that there was one art in which they already excelled.

> I mean the art of gardening, or, as I should choose to call it, the art of creating landscape. [And in a footnote he continues], I have not been able to please myself with a single term that will express ground laid out on principles of natural picturesque beauty, in

> contradistinction to symmetrical gardens, but I am very clear that the designer of modern improvements in *Landscape-gardens* (as I will call them for want of a happier appellation) ought by no means be confounded with the domestic called a *gardener* ... the projector I should propose to denominate a *Gardenist*.

There is something rather élitist about the sound of this, which is probably why he makes no mention at all of William Shenstone, who not only did not have a title, but had not even been to Eton. A modest, middle class, grammar-school boy, living on the outskirts of Birmingham, it is he nevertheless who is credited with the very first recorded use of the term *landscape-gardening* in his discerning and much earlier essay 'Unconnected Thoughts on Gardening'. And it was his own comparatively small garden, *The Leasowes*, near Halesowen, which so influenced Enville and Hagley, the estates of the Earl of Stamford and Sir George Lyttleton, and which was to win such world renown that it was visited, among multitudes of others, by two future US presidents, Adams and Jefferson, as well as by Samuel Johnson and the then-renowned poet, James Thomson. In his 'Essay on Pope' Joseph Warton called The Leasowes 'a fine example of practical poetry.'

That 'On Modern Gardening' was included in his *Anecdotes of Painting* indicates that Horace intended it to be a history, the history of a related *art*. And of course as a history it owes much to what had gone before it – in this case Addison, Pope and Thomas Whately. It is Pope's translation he uses in his account of the Garden of Alcinous in *The Odyssey* and he also quotes from 'The Epistle to Lord Burlington', one of the most influential statements made about landscape gardening in its time, and containing the famous direction:

> In all, let Nature never be forgot,

And also the delightful attack on excessive regularity:

> Grove nods at Grove, each Alley has a Brother,
> And half the Platform just reflects the other.

And behind Pope there is Addison who had mocked topiary in his *Spectator* essay of April 1711: 'Our trees rise in Cones, Globes and Pyramids. We see the Marks of the Scissors on every Plant and Bush.' It was he who first suggested that, 'There is something more bold and masterly in the rough, careless Strokes of Nature, than in the nice Touches and Embellishments of Art.' His also was that most fundamental proposal of all:

> Why may not a whole Estate be thrown into a kind of Garden by frequent Plantations, that may turn as much to the Profit, as the Pleasure of the owner ... Fields of corn make a pleasant Prospect, and if the Walks were a little taken care of that lie between them, if the natural Embroidery of the Meadows were kept and improved by some small additions of Art, and the several rows of Hedges set off by Trees and Flowers, that the Soil was capable of receiving, a Man might make a pretty Landskip of his own possessions.

This was a full half century before Horace began to embellish his own estate and make a pretty landskip of it.

As he had intended the work to be read as a history, 'strict impartiality' would, he said, be necessary, but these were the closing words of the essay, and he seems to have forgotten by that time that in his opening pages he had seen no reason why he should not have some fun at the expense of the French: 'When a Frenchman reads of the Garden of Eden, I do not doubt but that he concludes it was something approaching that of Versailles.' But, as we will see, patriotism was to play a fundamental role in what he was about to write.

That he should begin his history with the Garden of Eden is only natural, as, after all, the garden of Eden was only natural, and 'everything that was pleasant to the sight and good for food' grew in it. But after the Fall, poverty and necessity imposed their limitations and 'a slip of ground for a cabbage and a gooseberry bush' was all that the earliest gardens might have been. Even in Homer's age the renowned garden of Alcinous in *The Odyssey* was, he says, 'an enclosure of four acres, comprehending orchard, vineyard and kitchen garden, a stretch of luxury the world at that time had never beheld.'

There were exceptions. The Hanging Gardens of Babylon, 'unnatural and enriched by art' were 'a wanton instance of expense and labour.' Wealth, vanity and ostentation, we are persuaded, are at the core of all such things. Extravagance was also a feature of Rome and he cites Pliny's account of his garden, with its topiary, terraces, cascades and obelisks. And such could, he observes, serve for a description of any one of the gardens laid out on Dutch principles by the designers London and Wise during the reign of William III. They are thus made to sound like foreign impositions.

His hostility to such fashions is powerfully put and at length.

> Art ... in the hand of ostentatious wealth became the means of oppressing nature and the more it traversed the march of the latter, the more nobility thought its power was demonstrated ... every improvement that was made was but a step farther from nature ... the compass and square were of more use in plantations than the nurseryman.

What follows is not at all what we would expect. One man, we are told, one great man, realised that such gardens were 'unworthy of the almighty hand that planted the delights of paradise' and that man was John Milton. He, according to Horace, foresaw 'with prophetic eye' the future which modern gardening was to take and he quotes from *Paradise Lost* extracts which, he claims, 'could have been painted from Hagley or Stourhead.' Being blind, Milton had of course never seen anything of the like; it was instead his 'intellectual eye' and his 'boundless imagination' which told him 'how a plan might be disposed, that would embellish nature, and restore art to its proper office, the just improvement or imitation of it.'

Attention then switches to Sir William Temple, a contemporary of Milton, but almost his exact opposite, a Tory who served under Charles II. In his 'Upon the Gardens of Epicurus', Temple extolled the beauties of the Countess of Bedford's estate Moor Park in Hertfordshire and Horace quotes him at great length, so allowing him to damn himself out of his own mouth. To give a brief example: 'From this walk are three descents by many stone steps, in the middle and at each end, into a very large parterre. This is divided in quarters by gravel walks and adorned with two fountains and eight statues in the several quarters'. It is everything that Horace could not abide, 'How cold, how insipid, how tasteless ... it is his want of ideas, of imagination, of taste that I censure.' But Sir William was so enamoured of it that he even re-named his own estate Moor Park.

Sir William did concede that there might possibly be beauty of some kind in irregularity, saying that he had heard of such in China where it went by the name of *Sharawaggi*, a term it is thought he might have invented. Irregularity of this kind did have some appeal for Horace, but the suggestion that the English owed something to China was too much. His patriotism was aroused and he exploded the very idea of it in a long footnote: 'This is a blunder and the Chinese have passed to one extremity of absurdity, as the French and all antiquity had advanced to the other, both being equally remote from nature.'

At this point we at last come to modern gardening, 'Absurdity could go no further and the tide turned.' Credit for the first movements of this tide is given to Charles Bridgeman, a garden designer whose reputation has dwindled somewhat in more recent years, but who had been Royal Gardener to Queen Anne and who had played his part in the creation of both Stowe and Rousham. But his 'master stroke', according to Horace, had been the ha-ha, that ditch or fosse which had led to the eradication of boundary walls and fences and allowed gardens – his father's at Houghton among the first, he claims – to seem to blend in with the further landscape.

The greatest acclaim, however, goes to William Kent, who, while training as a landscape painter in Italy had caught the attention of the Duke of Burlington and returned with him to England where he assisted in the design of the Duke's gardens at Chiswick and later went on to create Lord Cobham's garden at Stowe.

The first thing Horace says about Kent is that he was 'painter enough to taste the charms of landscape' and later refers to the 'pencil of his imagination'. Likewise, 'The principles on which he worked were perspective, and light and shade.' As we have already observed, Horace always saw a connection between landscape painting and landscape gardening, so Kent, having been trained in the former and excelling in the latter, was looked upon as the personification of the ideal, and Horace's tribute to him has become almost proverbial: 'He leaped the fence and saw that all nature was a garden.' The sincerity of his praise is evident from its being not unqualified. He points out his debt to Pope and mocks him for once having planted dead trees in Kensington to give it 'greater truth'.

He also singles out Sir Henry Englefield's house in Berkshire on account of its 'prospect' by which he means not simply an extended view, but somewhere where there is activity. As he puts it with regard to the fashion for hermitages, ' ... it is almost comic to set aside a quarter of one's garden to be melancholy in. Prospect, animated prospect is the theatre that will always be the most frequented.' And his reply to Mann, when asked if his garden would also be gothic, was that *gloomth* was only for buildings, 'one's garden is to be nothing but riant.'

Generous tribute is also paid to his predecessor, Thomas Whately, whose 'Observations on Modern Gardening' had been published in 1770, but he is hesitant about Whately's tendency to lay down rules, not that he himself was not at times guilty of being assertive. On the topic of huge mansions, he asserts that earlier generations used to live surrounded by their extended families, but 'that method of living is now totally changed and yet the same superb palaces are still created, becoming a pompous solitude to the owner.' It is surprising he did not quote from Alexander Pope's 'Epistle to Burlington':

> Greatness, with Timon, dwells in such a draught
> As brings all Brobdignag before your thought.

> To compass this, his building is a Town,
> His pond an Ocean, his parterre a Down,
> Who but must laugh, the Master when he sees,
> A puny Insect, shiv'ring at a breeze!

The closing pages strike a note not only of patriotism but of optimism.

> We have given the true model of gardening to the world; let other countries mimic or corrupt our taste: but let it reign here on its verdant throne, original by its elegant simplicity, and proud of no other art than that of softening nature's harshness and copying her graceful touch.

It is an optimism which is carried over and back into landscape painting: 'If wood, water, groves, valleys, glades can inspire or poet or painter, this is the country, this is the age to produce them.'

'Capability' Brown is not mentioned and Horace seems to have had very little time for him. Writing to George Montagu in 1760 about Lord Anson's More-Park, he referred to the 'miracles' Brown had performed there: 'He has undulated the horizon in so many artificial mole-hills that it is full as unnatural as if it had been drawn with a rule and compass.' It may be that Brown is famous because he had a funny nickname and is the only landscape gardener most people have ever heard of. But what did he achieve? He destroyed some wonderful and elegant gardens, abolished parterres and flowers and colour and created 'natural landscapes' in a country which already abounded in such landscapes. If ever anyone is guilty of re-inventing the wheel, it is Mr Lancelot 'Capability' Brown.

Horace closes with tributes to the garden created by his cousin Henry Conway at Park Place and to the Vyne, the garden of his friend John Chute, tributes which cause us to realise that he has said nothing whatsoever of his own achievement at Strawberry Hill.

Students and historians of architecture are presented with few problems when they come to write about the structural development of Strawberry Hill as it is still all there, but the gardens have largely gone and we have no detailed maps, and written accounts, such as we have, thanks to Robert Dodsley, of The Leasowes. There are some attractive water colours by Barrow, Dobbyns and Farrington, but our impressions of what it was like and how it was constructed have to be put together from references over the years in Horace's letters. One of the earliest is a record of his visit to Houghton in 1736. He was not greatly enamoured of his father's palatial building, but he loved its garden: 'We have a charming garden, all wilderness; much adapted to my romantic inclinations.' That his response was emotional rather than aesthetic is worth noting, as his reason for buying Strawberry Hill was not initially the house but its 'Prospect'. Even before he moved in, his letter to Horace Mann in Florence is chiefly about the location.

> The prospect is as delightful as possible, commanding the river, the town, and Richmond Park; and being situated on three little meadows, where I have some Turkish sheep, and two cows, all studied in their colour for becoming the view.

It was not until January 1750 that he told him, 'I am going to build a little Gothic castle at Strawberry Hill.' His early thoughts centred on the garden. He had, as he indicated in his 'Essay', recognised the need to give such an undertaking careful consideration before any work was actually carried out. It was not until eighteen months later, during the Christmas of 1784, that he tells Mann:

> I am extremely busy here planting; I have got four more acres, which makes my territory prodigious ... and I am making a terrace the whole breadth of my garden on the brow of a natural hill, with meadows at the foot, and commanding the river, the village, Richmond Hall and the Park.

Thus the 'prospect' was established and secured.

It is clear that he really enjoyed gardening as we can tell from the self-mockery in a letter to Conway.

> My present and sole occupation is planting, in which I have made great progress, and talk very learnedly with nurserymen, except that now and then a lettuce run to seed overturns all my botany, and I have more than once taken it for a curious West Indian flowering shrub.

But by 1755 we learn from a letter to George Montagu that his own nursery can supply him with 'three Chinese arbor vitaes, a dozen of the New England pines.' What is more surprising is how knowledgeable he had become and that some of the hands-on work was being carried out by his own hands:

> and six acacias, the gentlest tree of all, but you must take care to plant them in a first row, and where they will be well sheltered, for the least wind tears and breaks them to pieces ... They are exceeding small, as I have but lately taken to propagating myself, but they will travel more safely.

In the early years, the positioning and planting of trees was a major concern. Judiciously done it would allow him to screen views he didn't want, and to frame those he did. An amusing change occurs as the years pass. In 1748 he is complaining of how slowly they grow, 'it is extremely inconvenient to my natural impatience.' But two decades later, 'My trees flourish so exuberantly that I am every day clearing away and every bough lopped lets in new verdure, gaiety and prospect.' That word again.

Our clearest picture of what he achieved comes in the long and detailed letter he sent to Mann in June of 1753. From it we learn that to the east was a 'serpentine wood of all kinds of trees, flowering shrubs and flowers.' And through this serpentine wood, a serpentine path went meandering making the limited area seem bigger than it was and giving his visitors unexpected views at its different twists and turns.

Waiting for such visitors at the end of their tour was an oak bench, designed by Bentley, and shaped like a scallop shell. It was erected to the memory of Horace's mother and was a substantial structure, big enough to sit three ladies on one occasion: the Duchesses of Hamilton and Richmond and Lady Ailesbury – 'There never was so pretty a sight as to see them all three sitting in the shell.'

The shell bench was not the only structure in the garden. There was a cottage and a chapel, both substantial buildings in themselves to judge from illustrations, and latterly a tea-room and a little library for visitors to rest in when they had completed their tour. These features, together with an ornate garden gate and a Gothic bridge over Cross Deep Stream, were all architecturally in keeping, unlike Stowe where a Roman Temple, a Gothic Towers and a Chinese Pagoda all stood within the same sight-line.

Furthermore, in keeping perhaps with monastic tradition, there was a pond – Pa-Yang he called it – where he bred goldfish, some no doubt for that indoor tub which brought about the untimely demise of Selima. The goldfish were obviously a great success, as in the summer of 1753 he offered to send some to George Montagu: 'You would be enthralled by our fishing; instead of nets and rods, lines and worms, we use nothing but a pail and a basin and a tea-strainer.'

It is easy enough to list the physical features of the garden in this way, but it does little to tell us what it was *like*. Fortunately, Horace himself does so in one of the happiest letters he ever wrote. It was to Montagu and dated 'June 10th 1765. Eleven at night.'

> I am just come out of the garden in the most oriental of all evenings, and from breathing odours beyond those of Araby. The acacias, which the Arabians have the sense to worship, are covered with blossoms, the honeysuckles dangle from every tree in festoons, the seringas are thickets of sweets, and the new-cut hay of the field in the garden tempers the balmy gales with simple freshness ...

He once wrote admiringly of William Kent, 'Mahomet imagined an Elysium, but Kent created many.' At Strawberry Hill, Horace himself certainly came very close to creating one.

8

THE POLITICIAN

FOR MANY YOUNG MEN OF NOBLE families, entering Parliament in the eighteenth century was simply what one did. It was not something they regarded as a career, nor were they motivated by a burning desire to do something for their country. If anything, their motive was to try and get something out of it – some lucrative sinecure. In July 1740, while still in Florence, Horace wrote to his cousin Henry Conway, 'You are to come back to stand for some place ... 'tis a sort of thing I should do too, but it is a sort of thing I have no mind to do.' The very term 'some place' shows the casual attitude they took to it. Indeed Horace was still in Italy when he was elected MP for Callington in Cornwall, a constituency he 'represented' for over ten years without once even visiting it.

It was very different when his father was elected for Castle Rising in Norfolk in 1701 at the age of 25. Politically ambitious from the outset, he became a member of a committee within three days, and when the accession of George I brought about the fall of the Tory party and a new Whig government, he rose rapidly. By 1721 he had become First Lord of the Treasury,

Chancellor of the Exchequer and Leader of the House of Commons. And though the term did not then officially exist, he was *de facto* Prime Minister, a position he held until 1742, a record which no subsequent leader has come close to.

A commanding personality and a powerful speaker, Robert Walpole was also a consummate tactician with a knowledge of parliamentary procedure which often enabled him to outwit and outmanoeuvre his opponents, but it was his skill in handling the country's financial affairs which was his chief asset. He managed to restore fiscal confidence after the chaotic collapse of the South Sea Bubble and to stabilise the National Debt. Added to this was his determination to keep the country out of costly European wars and so ensure that taxes remained low and trade could prosper. A more dubious skill, however, was his management of honours and offices which trod a fine line between patronage and bribery.

The careers of political leaders rarely end happily and after 21 years Parliament began to turn on him. In 1740 he could not prevent the country from being dragged into the War of Austrian Succession but he gave the Duke of Newcastle due warning, 'The war is yours; I wish you well of it.' And predicting, 'They are now ringing their bells, they will soon be ringing their hands.'

Matters quickly became personal. The threat of impeachment was in the air. The opposition tried to set up a secret commission 'to investigate persons and papers.' His sons were suggesting resignation and when another vote of confidence was lost he did so, in February 1742.

News of his father's predicament and ill health had brought Horace home to London in September 1741. He had not seen him for two and a half years, but initially fun came before family and politics. He was a young man. He had been away a long time. There were friends to be caught up with, parties to go to; news and gossip to be exchanged. But when Parliament re-convened in December, he rose to make an impassioned speech in Sir Robert's defence. It is one of very few he did make to the House and is preserved in a letter he sent to Horace Mann.

> While the attempts for the enquiry were made in general terms, I should have thought it presumptuous of me to stand up ... but when the attack grows more personal, it grows my duty to oppose it, more particularly lest I be suspected of an ingratitude which my heart disdains ... for twenty years together, no crime could be solemnly alleged against him, and since his dismission he has seen a majority rise to defend his character in that very House of Commons in which a majority had overturned his power. As therefore, Sir, I must think him innocent, I stand up to protect him from injustice.

Sir Robert's health began to fail and he left London for Houghton. Although, as we have seen, Horace never really liked the place, he spent a good deal of time there caring for him, and the warmth of their relationship can be seen in the closing words of a letter Sir Robert sent him in July 1744: 'All the disagreeable symptoms I had are gone and this I verily believe will make you partake in my pleasures ... but we all love to please ourselves, and may it always be in your power to make yourself as happy as I wish you, for I am most truly, Yours affectly.'

His grief at his father's death is evident in his letter to Mann: 'A death is only to be felt, never to be talked over by those it touches!' And from that moment, he never ceases, in memory and honour of his father one might say, to be concerned with and by the political situation. Both *Aedes Walpolianae* and *Royal and Noble Authors,* we have seen have a political sub-text and contain explicit celebrations of his father's achievements.

The rise of the Whig party can be dated from the Glorious Revolution of 1688. It was they who engineered the ousting of the autocratic, Catholic James II and invited the Protestant William III to take the throne, but he was to take it very much on their terms, terms which, first and foremost, meant the supremacy of Parliament. This, the defence of liberty as against the Tories favouring of adherence to the royal prerogative, may be seen as the root difference between them, but they were not separate and distinct parties in today's understanding of the term. Disagreements and factions existed within both groups and the factions were often better known by the name of the leading figure to whom the others were indebted or dependent. Hence there are references to the Rockinghams, the Bedfords and the Graftons. Horace was as much opposed to what he called 'the confederacy of great lords' as he was to the royal prerogative and declared to Fox in 1765 that he 'enjoyed the liberty of pleasing himself without being tied to a party.'

The fundamental beliefs to which he held so firmly were demonstrated even from the decorations in his bedroom. 'On one side of my bed,' he told George Montagu in a letter of 1756 'I have hung MAGNA CARTA and the Warrant for the King's execution, on which I have written MAGNA CHARTA, as I believe that without the latter, the former by this time would be of very little importance.'

The occasions on which he wrote and acted in defence of liberty are many and various. He voted against the more brutal clauses in the Mutiny Bill and supported the Act which permitted the naturalisation of the Jews, an Act later repealed by 'superstitious bigots' which , as he said, 'demonstrated how much the age, enlightened as it is called, was still enslaved to the grossest and most vulgar prejudices.'

In his Memoirs and letters there is both anger and passion when he recounts the events leading up to the execution of Admiral Byng. We can safely say that Horace never joined in with the London mob chanting, 'Swing, swing, Admiral Byng', but he did initially go along with the general view that he was culpable. In his *Memoirs* he says, 'I was carried away with the multitude in believing that he had not done his duty.' But once he had read Byng's own defence, he realised that the Admiralty and the Government were using him as a scapegoat to cover their own crass ineptitude. He now saw him as 'one marked for sacrifice by a set of Ministers who meant to direct on him the vengeance of a brutalized and enraged nation.' There was nothing personal in his reaction; it was a matter of principle. As he told Mann:

> I never knew poor Byng enough to bow to – but the great doubtfulness of his crime and the extraordinariness of his sentence, the persecution of his enemies who sacrifice him for their own guilt, and the rage of a blinded nation, have called forth all my pity for him – his enemies triumph but who can envy the triumph of murder?

It came at an awkward time for Horace as he was not then an MP, having just resigned his seat for Castle Rising, but had not yet been elected for King's Lynn. He needed help, and managed to persuade Rockingham to appeal to the Speaker of the House for a two-week stay of execution, but in the end the Lords threw the appeal out, leaving Horace with the sad realisation that he had only been 'instrumental in protracting his misery for a fortnight by what I had meant as the kindest thing I could do.'

His account of the execution, both in his *Memoirs* and in his letter to Mann is such that one could believe he had been present and witnessed it himself.

> He desired to be shot on the quarter-deck, not where common malefactors are; came out at twelve, sat down on a chair, for he would not kneel, and refused to have his face covered, that his countenance might show whether he feared death; but being told that it might frighten his executioners, he submitted, saying, 'If it will frighten them, let it be done. They would not frighten me.' His eyes were bound, he gave the signal at once, received one shot through the head, another through the heart, and fell.

In supporting Byng he was, as we have seen, defending the liberty of someone he hardly knew; equally his heart went out on another occasion to a group of people he could never possibly have known – the slaves in the American plantations. Telling Mann in 1750 of the debate in Parliament, he was blunt about it:

> We have this fortnight been pondering methods to make more effective that horrid traffic of selling negroes. It has appeared to us that six and forty thousand of these wretches are sold every year to our plantations alone! – it chills the blood.

And this was 83 years before the passing of the Slavery Abolition Act. During that time many had felt that the economy could not survive without slaves, but writing to Mann in 1752 he was again adamant:

> I don't care a farthing for the interests of merchants. Soldiers and sailors who are knocked on the head, peasants plundered and butchered, are to my eyes as valuable as a lazy, luxurious set of men who hire others to acquire riches for them.

Of course as an aristocrat of independent means, it was easy for him to adopt such an attitude to trade. Yet he was seemingly unaware that women and children were working in appallingly dangerous conditions in the mines and mills of his own country. The industrial revolution passed him by – or rather he passed by it. Machines? Yes, as he once remarked to Hannah More, they might be used for making sugar, so the poor negroes could be saved from working. But as Lytton Strachey concluded, 'He departed, happily unconscious that the whole system of his existence was doomed to annihilation – elegantly unaware of the implications of the spinning-jenny.'

But his compassion for the slaves working in the plantations presented a problem when their masters made their own bid for liberty. Writing to Mason in 1774 he declared, 'If all the black slaves were in rebellion, I should have no doubt in choosing my side, but I scarce wish perfect freedom to merchants who are the bloodiest of tyrants. I should think the souls of the Africans would sit heavy on the swords of the Americans.'

In a remarkable entry in his *Memoirs* as early as 1754, Horace seems to have had a premonition of the troubles which were to follow. Describing how Newcastle exalted the dignity of the crown at the expense the colonies and aware of the haughtiness with which they were being treated, he wrote 'suspicions had long been conceived of their meditating to throw off their dependence on their mother country.' And again in 1770, writing to Mann, 'I have many visions about that country ... which is growing too mighty to be kept in subjection to half a dozen exhausted nations in Europe.'

Serious trouble had begun in 1765 with the passing of the notorious Stamp Act. The justice of the colonists' reaction of 'No taxation without representation' would have reminded some of John Hampden's refusal in 1635 to accept King Charles's demand for Ship Money, one of those deciding moments which were part of the slide into civil war. Horace was as opposed to war as was his father. 'Setting both countries at variance,' he insisted, 'would lead to a scene of long and terrible calamity for both England and her colonies', adding 'It is the kindest way of ruling men to govern them as they will be governed, not as they ought to be governed.'

Then in 1773 the *Boston Tea Party* took place. Calling it so is to trivialise the event and Horace for one does not seem to have taken it seriously. The Bostonians, he told Mann, 'will not drink tea with our Parliament.' There is a comic side to it when we think of them dressed up as Mohawk Indians and giving war-whoops as they ran down to the harbour, but throwing 342 chests of tea into the ocean was not funny, especially not for the merchants who had shipped it. Interfering with trade is a serious matter, far more serious than politics and Lord North saw nothing at all funny in it – 'Convince your colonies that you are able and not afraid to control them, and, depend upon it, obedience will be the result of your deliberations.' Strong words, but delivered from a position of weakness.

An additional ten thousand British troops were landed on American soil and advanced on Concord where it was thought 'the rebels', as they were now called, had stored their weaponry, but they were stopped short at Lexington Green, where a contingent led by General Gage was driven back with loss of nearly 300 men. Worse was to follow at the battle of Bunker's Hill when British losses exceeded a thousand officers and men. It was a national humiliation, which Horace caught most aptly: 'Our conduct has been that of pert children: we have thrown a pebble at a mastiff, and are surprised that it is not frightened.'

George III was still clinging to the illusion that 'normality' would be restored, but even he saw that it would entail more bloodshed: 'The die is now cast; the colonies must either submit or triumph.' But Thomas Paine's pamphlet 'Common Sense' was telling the Americans early in 1776 that, 'The King has shown himself such an inveterate enemy to liberty and discovered such a thirst for arbitrary power that he must be resisted.' A few months later the Declaration of Independence was signed. In effect it was all over. It dragged on however as these things tend to do, and we sense the total despair in Horace's letter to Mann of February 1778.

> [Parliament] solicits peace with the states of America; it haggles on no terms, it acknowledges Congress, or anybody that pleases to treat; it confesses errors; it disclaims taxation, desires commerce, hopes for assistance ... allows the independence of America ... To leap at once from an obstinacy of four years to a total concession of everything, to stoop so low without hope of being forgiven; who can understand such a transformation? All that remains certain is that America is not only lost, but given up. We must no longer give ourselves continental airs! I fear, even our trident will

find it has lost a considerable prong. I have lived long, but never saw such a day as last Tuesday!

What was worse, his prediction that 'instead of peace, we must expect war' was to come true; England was soon at war again with France and fearful of an invasion, but no one could have foreseen what was about to happen there. Horace always regarded himself as a republican. 'Republicans,' he wrote, 'may prove objectionable as usurpers; yet republicanism as it tends to promote liberty, and patriotism as far as it tends to preserve or restore it, are still godlike principles.' But the French Revolution went far beyond anything he could have imagined, let alone countenance. As they unfold, the letters he wrote between 1771 and 1794 tell us more about those eventful years than could any history written after they had come to an end. They begin with an account of the country's financial collapse: 'The king's tradesman are ruined, his servants starving and you never saw so great a nation in so disgraceful a position.' Horace bewails the 'ruinous condition of the palaces ... it rains in upon the pictures.' But, in contrast, on a visit in 1775 he saw Marie Antoinette, 'a statue of beauty ... grace itself when she moves.' Even a reference to the release of prisoners from the Bastille has its light-hearted moments, 'One man refused his liberty; he said he had been prisoner fifteen years that the King had fed and lodged him and he would not quit the Bastille unless they would give him half his pension.' But by 1789 he is sensing trouble: 'No man living is more devoted to liberty than I am, yet blood is a terrible price to pay for it!' At first he seems uncertain how to react to the fall of the Bastille: 'I do not pretend to foresee what will happen ... chance and folly are apt to contradict calculation.' He declares some sympathy with the King and hopes that what is happening 'is but a bloody fashion, and momentary, like their other modes.' We begin to see the aristocrat in Horace coming to the fore when he describes the revolutionaries as 'having no education at all, but have been debased, brutalized by a long train of superstition and oppression.'

And then, 'The uproar has begun' but 'into what such a chaos will subside, it would be silly to attempt to guess.' How could anyone have predicted 'fifteen hundred persons, probably more, butchered on the 10th in the space of eight hours.'

Historians must at least aim at a degree of objectivity, but in Horace's contemporary accounts the emotional response is still there, indeed is foremost, and brief quotation can do little to suggest the impact made by an extensive reading of these letters. They are among his major achievements. We share his horror at the execution of the King and Queen and can sense his feeling of emotional exhaustion at the news of Robespierre's eventual fall. The outrage he felt was still there, we remember, in his Addenda to his *Catalogue of Royal and Noble Authors.*

> N.B. This addition was written before the Revolution in France in 1789; since when the follies of that nation have soured and plunged into the most execrable barbarity, immorality, injustice, usurpation and tyranny; have rejected God himself and deified human monsters have dared to call this mass of unheard crimes 'giving liberty to mankind' by atheism and massacres!

Those who will persist in seeing Horace as an effeminate dilettante have to ignore the seriousness with which he approached the changing political situations of his time. It is certainly true that he showed very little interest in the constituencies he represented. On one occasion when he did feel obliged to visit

King's Lynn, when he was given the freedom of the city during the election of 1761, he clearly hated all the jollifications it involved.

> Think of me the subject of a mob, who was scarce ever before in a mob, addressing them in the town hall, riding at the head of two thousand people ... dining with above two hundred of them, amid bumpers, huzzas, songs, and tobacco, and finishing with country dancing at a ball and sixpenny whisk! I have borne it all cheerfully ...

It sounds dreadful and in all probability most of his colleagues, if they had been as honest, would have expressed the same sentiments. However, when he relinquished the seat in 1768, his letter to the mayor is notable for its courtesy and in it he makes a claim which it is unlikely that many of his colleagues in the House could in all honesty have made: that he had never asked for or received a personal favour, nor had his votes ever been dictated by any outside influence whatsoever. On the face of it, it might appear that Horace had had no parliamentary career at all. He held no office. He instigated no legislation, spoke on perhaps no more than half a dozen occasions and being of a somewhat unprepossessing appearance, with a high-pitched, weak voice, he would have cut no figure in a debate. But in private and on the back-benches, his was a voice which counted. Known as a man of principle and ideas, he was listened to and had influence. It was an influence which he chiefly channelled through his cousin Henry Conway, who had all the outer qualities Horace lacked, but was himself certainly not a man of ideas or of imagination.

Horace had long idolised his younger cousin. In an early part of his *Memoirs* he credits him with 'superior understanding' and 'being one of the most agreeable and solid speakers in Parliament, to which the beauty of his person and the harmony of his voice, did remarkably contribute.' In 1743, he had been prepared to give him almost all the money he had to enable him to marry and in 1763 he again did all he could to help him. The trouble began with the publication in the *North Briton* of John Wilkes' attack on the King's speech at the prorogation of Parliament. He was arrested on a general warrant and sent to The Tower, but released on the grounds of a breach of parliamentary privilege. When the constitutional legality of general warrants became an issue, the government was in full support of the King's action, but Walpole and a small minority believing that a principle of liberty was at stake, voted against the motion and he persuaded Conway to vote with them. The King regarded it as a personal affront and was outraged. There was nothing he could do about a backbencher, but Conway held a Court position as Groom of the Bedchamber and was also a general with a distinguished military record. He had fought at Culloden under Cumberland. The King's response was swift, decisive and devastating; Conway was deprived of both his court post and of his command.

Horace blamed himself for this personal disaster and immediately offered him £6,000, all his invested capital, to make up for his loss of income. Again Conway declined the offer, but Horace did not stop at that. He published a pamphlet *On the Late Dismissal of a General Officer* which concluded, 'The public is hurt, if the rights of parliament are violated, and if punishment, which is only due to crimes, is inflicted on incorruptible honesty and conscientious virtue.'

Initially this changed nothing, but in 1765 when Grenville's government fell, a new administration was formed under the Marquis of Rockingham, and Conway was re-instated as Secretary of State. It was an event which would have entitled Horace to feel that he would receive some form of recognition. He would never have accepted a ministerial appointment, but would have liked the opportunity of refusing one. To his chagrin, he learned that after all he had done for Conway, his name had not even come up for discussion. It is quite possible that Conway, in his own dull way of thinking, reasoned that as he knew Horace would not accept any offer, it was pointless making him one. If so, he didn't understand Horace, who made his hurt feelings very plain in his *Memoirs* which were not to be read until long after his death.

> But what could excuse this neglect in Mr Conway? For him I had sacrificed everything; for him I had been injured, oppressed, calumniated. The foundation of his own fortune, and almost every step of his fortune, he owed solely to me. How thoroughly soever he knew my sentiments, was a compliment at least not due to me? ... Such failure of friendship, or, to call it by its truer name, such insensibility, could not but shock a heart at once so tender and so proud as mine. His ensuing conduct completely opened my eyes.

One benefit to come out of Conway's new appointment was that at Horace's request his friend Mann in Florence was promoted to the rank of envoy. Horace himself, perhaps in something of a fit of pique, set off for an extended stay in Paris, telling Montague, 'when I meet with ingratitude, I take a short leave of it and its host.'

It was in Paris where he met Mme du Deffand, who was to play such an important role in his life for the next fifteen years. Conway, still failing to understand the situation, had done his best with 'complaints, entreaties and reproaches' to persuade him to stay, and was left feeling, doubtless to Horace's satisfaction, that he had been *abandoned*. But on Horace's return the following year their friendship was resumed with no obvious recriminations. His time in Parliament was coming to a close. As early as 1762 he had wearily complained to Mann, 'For twenty years I have been looking at parties, factions, changes and struggles. Do you wonder I am tired when I have seen them so often acted over and performed by the same *dramatis personis?*' He finally resigned his seat in 1768.

Looking back over Horace's active years in the Commons, we see a man of compassionate and liberal views, selfless, totally loyal to his friends and content to let others take the credit for proposals he had suggested. With qualities as noble as these, it was just as well that he had never set out with any real political ambition.

He may have given up his seat in the Commons in 1768, but his involvement in politics did not stop there; he continued with the 'Memoirs' which he had begun in 1751. The story of their eventual publication has a delightful element of romance to it. In August 1796, seven months before his death, he wrote a memorandum endorsed, 'Not to be opened till after my Will'. In it he declared that in the Library of Strawberry Hill there was a wainscot chest marked with an A. It was to be strongly bound and sealed by his executors and delivered to Hugh Conway Selwyn who was to hold it in safe-keeping for the first son of Lady Waldegrave to reach the age of 25. The key to it, he wrote, adding to the sense of mystery, was in one of the cupboards of the Green Closet in the Blue Breakfast Room and was to be given to Lady Waldegrave. It was duly presented to its new owner in 1810, but he seems to have had little interest in it, not opening it until 1813 and then promptly passing on to his friend Lord Holland, a classical scholar, all its 23 folio volumes of memoirs and journals. Lord Holland set about editing (and censoring) the journals, but it was 1822 before they were published. There is no clear statement that Horace wanted them published, but enough evidence in the text to show that that was what he intended. The volume for 1752 begins, 'I sit down to resume a task for which I fear posterity will condemn the author at the same time that they feel their curiosity gratified.' He proved to be right on both counts.

The opening pages of the 1751 volume make for rather dull reading unless you know who the noble politicians were, who they were related to and what they were up to, but then we come across a passing reference to a Miss Vane, 'a Maid of Honour, who was willing to cease to be so upon the first opportunity.' The wit, the brevity and the malice! This is a Horace Walpole we know.

The politicians and the majority of the political events would already have been met with by readers of his letters, particularly those to Mann, but whereas those letters showed some discretion, here such niceties do not bother him. His tone is far more Hogarthian, and in a Postscript he freely admits that, 'Many will be offended at the liberty I have taken in painting men as they are and will dislike meeting such unflattered portraits of their heroes or their relatives.' In his defence he pointed out that, 'The scenes I described passed in the highest life, soil the vices like.' He claimed he had been equally blunt in relating the frailties of his friends and there may be some slight truth in this. He certainly never spared his uncle: 'a buffoon and avaricious.' But nothing equals the character assassination he handed out to those who had been involved in his father's downfall, and especially the Duke of Newcastle. 'His person was not naturally despicable; his incapacity, his mean soul, and the general low opinion of him, grew to make it appear ridiculous ... he had no pride but infinite self-love...There was no expense he was not addicted to but generosity ... He was a Secretary of State without intelligence, a Duke without money, a man of infinite intrigue ... a Minister hated and despised by his master.'

All this came as a shock to the first readers of the 'Memoirs' and certainly did damage his reputation. An unsigned review in the *Literary Gazette* of April 1822 complained of the, 'Premeditated cruelty of writing these Memoirs, and consigning them to future generations, blackening as they do the past age, is not to be contemplated without feelings of indignation, if not of horror.' And in the same month the *Quarterly* deplored 'the injuries done to private character by attributing the lowest and basest motives to almost every person whom he happens to mention.'

His strictures on Lord Hardwicke do make us pause and think. ' ... a man of low birth and of lower principles. He was a creature of the Duke of Newcastle ... In the House of Lords he was laughed at; in the Commons despised.' As Henry Hawkins, in his memoirs, asks, if this be true, how could it be possible that for fifty years he held so high a rank? However, what we have to recognise is that Horace knew these men personally; he lived among them and asserts that, 'Whoever knows the interior of affairs, must be sensible to how many more events the faults of statesmen give birth, than are produced by their good intentions.' And few men knew the *interior of affairs* better than Horace. Hawkins may have shared others' reservations, but could not resist the 'wit and brilliance of the satire', recognising that 'What is good in it could come from no other author than Horace Walpole himself.'

As usual, Horace plays down his achievement, claiming 'I am no historian. I write casual memoirs, I draw characters, I preserve anecdotes which my superiors, the historian of Britain may enchase into their weighty annals or to pass over at their pleasure.' This may be true, but it is only partly true. As his 'superiors' have long recognised there is real history in these Memoirs. It is here that we are given the full account of the fate of Admiral Byng – full because Horace himself was, albeit reluctantly, involved in it. Of the falling-out between the King and the Duke of Cumberland, he says, 'I have dwelt minutely on the circumstances of this history … ' And *minutely* is the word. The detail is precise, 'At nine, the hour the King punctually goes to play [cards] in the apartment of Princess Emily, the Duke went to her.' This is history in close-up and never more so than in his account of the relationship between Lord Bute and the Princess Dowager.

> The eagerness of the Pages of the Backstairs to let her know whenever Lord Bute arrived, a mellowness in her German accent as often as she spoke to him and a more than usual swimmingness in her eyes, contributed to dispel the ideas that had been conceived of the rigour of her widowhood.

As he remarked on another occasion, he could not see how history could be faithful if it was always solemn, and solemnity was not something he allowed to intrude too often into his life. What we treasure are the passing observations he drops in, such as his assessment of The Lords: 'They look on themselves as distinct from the rest of the nation ... as fond of their privileges, as the King of his prerogative, they are attentive to retain them, and deem the rights of the people rather an encroachment than a common interest.' When he inherited the title of Earl of Orford in 1791 he did not take his seat in the Lords.

Horace was an integral part of the history, 'intimately connected with many of the chief actors', as he put it, and so nearer the truth than 'spectators'. It is not altogether surprising therefore that he should include an account of himself in the assessment. He begins by claiming that he was, 'without the least tincture of ambition.' If we take *ambition* here to refer solely to the world of politics and government, then it is true that he never sought any kind of public appointment, but he wanted to be *known*. No one would have built such an extravaganza as Strawberry Hill or have written *The Castle of Otranto* if they wanted to remain quietly unnoticed in the background. And in the political sphere he never undervalued his own importance.

> ... my counsels might have been more serviceable to my country and to my friends if they had been more followed, they were calculated to produce neither glory nor profit to myself, and were much oftener neglected than listened to. Nor should they be remembered here, if many miscarriages had not accrued from the neglect of them, as was felt and confessed by those to whom they had been suggested.

And these were claims he prefaced by assuring his readers, 'It is to gratify no vanity that I relate them.' Who, one wonders, is he trying to convince?

Warmth of feeling might have been in short supply in these

pages, and yet, for all his declared Republicanism, Horace could be generous in his attitude to both Georges. Of George II he wrote, 'Full of years and glory, he died without a pang and with no reverse. He left his family firmly established on a long-disputed throne.' And at the outset he was happy to welcome the new King, telling George Montagu that, 'The young King has all the appearance of being amiable. There is great grace to his temper, much dignity and extreme good nature.' Later, however, his views changed: 'He was unfeeling, insincere, cunning and trifling. Nature had given him the first quality and the last. His mother had taught him the second, and practice the third. He was rather silly than a fool.'

It is this waspishness of his character sketches which gives us the greatest enjoyment; though brutality might be a more appropriate word for what he had to say about Samuel Johnson.

> Johnson was an odious and mean character ... arrogant, self-sufficient, and over-bearing by nature ... His manners were sordid, supercilious, and brutal, his style ridiculously bombast and vicious; and, in one word, with all the pedantry he had all the gigantic littleness of a country schoolmaster.

With the exception of Gray (and there are reservations even there) Horace had a poor opinion of most contemporary writers. Richardson's novels he dismissed as, 'those deplorably tedious lamentations.' And of *Tristram Shandy* he wrote, 'It makes one smile two or three times at the beginning, but in recompense makes one yawn for two hours.' The antithesis is so Augustan; it comes with all the snap and bite of one of Pope's couplets, and the irony of *in recompense* is devastating.

Sir Leslie Stephen has given us a splendid image for these pen portraits: 'As in *The Castle of Otranto* the portraits of our respectable old ancestors, which have been hanging in gloomy repose upon the wall, suddenly step from their frames and for some brief space assume a spectral vitality.' It is hard to resist the temptation to go on quoting from the delights that Matthew Hodgart gathered together in his *Selection,* but his final page cannot be omitted. Writing of the Dowager Princess and her youngest son, the Duke of Gloucester, Horace tells us:

> She thought him insuperably dull, nor was he bright: one day in his childhood she ridiculed him before his brothers and sisters, and bade them laugh at the fool. He sat silent and thoughtful. She said, 'What! now are you sullen?' He replied, No, he was thinking. 'Thinking,' replied his mother, with scorn; 'and pray what are you thinking of?' He answered, 'I was thinking what I should feel if I had a son as unhappy as you make me!'

Now it is hard to know how he could have overheard such a sad and personal moment. It seems more likely that he is passing on some gossip, but the way in which he captures the event and especially the timing of the boy's reply reminds us that as well as being a very able historian and raconteur, Horace was also a novelist of some note.

9

GOTHIC TALES

'TIMOR MORTIS CONTURBAT ME' WAS THE doleful refrain William Dunbar penned in his 'Lament for the Makers' towards the end of the fifteenth century and five hundred years later Philip Larkin was still doing little to lessen our conturbation with poems such as his 'Aubade':

> The sure extinction that we travel to
> And shall be lost in always. Not to be here,
> Not to be anywhere,
> And soon; nothing more terrible, nothing more true.

Death and the fear of death have always been among the foremost struts of our literature. Few things more bleak can ever have been written than Lear's reaction to the death of Cordelia. 'Why should a dog, a horse, a rat, have life/ And thou no breath at all?' Or Claudio's squeamish lament in *Measure For Measure*:

> Ay, but to die, and go we know not where:
> To lie in cold obstruction and to rot.

It still gives us the shudders.

Yet death seems to have dropped briefly below the poetic horizon during what we call The Age of Reason. It hardly features at all in the work of Dryden and Pope and while Boswell frequently tells us that Johnson was terrified by the very thought of death, it rarely features in his essays. The dip, however, was only temporary and when feelings began to contend with rationalism, so it made a come-back, slowly at first but gathering force until it reached a positive crescendo of gloom in the 1740s with Edward Young's nine books of 'Night Thoughts' (1742) and Blair's 'The Grave' (1743)

> Strange things, the neighbours say, have happened here;
> Wild shrieks have issued from the hollow tombs;
> Dead men have come again and walked about,
> And the great bell has tolled unrung, untouched.

The 'Graveyard Poets', as they came to be called, certainly set the scene. But that was poetry where such flights of fancy were all very well, but the new fiction was concerned with the actualities of here and now: the social realism – grim though it often was – of Defoe and Fielding. Death had little part to play in it and fancy none whatsoever. Yet Horace Walpole managed to combine the two in 1764 with *The Castle of Otranto.*

He explained its genesis in a letter to the Rev William Cole on 9th March 1765:

> I waked one morning in the beginning of last June from a dream of which all I could recover was that I had thought myself in an ancient castle (a very natural dream for a head so filled like mine with Gothic story) and that on the uppermost banister of a great staircase I saw a gigantic hand in armour. In the evening I sat

down and began to write, without knowing in the least what I intended to say or relate. The work grew on my hands, and I grew fond of it – add that I was glad to think of anything rather than politics - in short I was so engrossed with my tale which I completed in less than two months.

The tale was *The Castle of Otranto,* which has come to be seen as one of the most influential English novels of the second half of the eighteenth century. It is interesting that he should have said that he wanted to think of anything rather than politics, as two of the story's major themes are tyranny and the rights of succession, two dominant Hanoverian issues. Horace's mind, even in his dreams, it would seem, was seldom unoccupied by politics.

Although he said that it was very natural for him to dream of a castle, and would later conclude his *Description of the Villa at Strawberry Hill* by saying that, ' ... it was the scene that inspired the author of the *Castle of Otranto',* the two had little in common. Otranto had none of the cheerful, cosy and brightly-coloured rooms of Strawberry Hill. And some decades later, when he was describing to his friend Mme du Deffand a visit he had made to Cambridge, he wrote, 'Entering one of the colleges [It was probably Trinity] I found myself in the courtyard of my own castle. The towers, the gateways, the chapel, the great hall corresponded with it exactly. The idea of that college had stayed in my head without me realising it and had served unconsciously as a model for my castle, so that I really seemed to be entering into Otranto.'

In *Otranto* Horace could be said to have turned upside down the whole idea of the *castle.* Castles had long been regarded as places of safety which kept one's enemies *out,* but Otranto was a place riddled with danger, a place people tried desperately hard to escape *from* – a nightmare place of guilty secrets and secret passages. It became the archetype of what Catherine Morland was expecting when she entered Northanger Abbey.

Published on Christmas Eve in 1764 and printed not by the Strawberry Hill Press but by Lowndes of Fleet Street, there was nothing to suggest that *The Castle of Otranto* had anything to do with Horace Walpole. The title page declared it to be a translation by William Marshall from the original Italian. At that point Horace was not even aware that there was an actual castle in Otranto until his friend Lady Craven sent him a drawing of such a place in 1786, twenty-two years later. And William Marshall just happened to be the name of an engraver mentioned in passing in a letter which Cole had written to him shortly before he completed the novel.

The reason for all this subterfuge was, again, Horace's abiding fear of ridicule, as Sir Walter Scott recognised in the Introduction to his edition of 1811.

> Mr Walpole, being uncertain of the reception which a work upon so new a plan might experience from the world, and not caring, perhaps, to encounter the ridicule which would have attended its failure, the Castle of Otranto was ushered into the world as a translation from the Italian.

But there is also the possibility that Horace was astutely and knowingly logging in to the marketing possibilities of a new literary trend. One of the most significant events of this trend having been the publication in 1762 of Bishop Richard Hurd's *Letters on Chivalry and Romance* which Horace had certainly read. In it Hurd argued that medieval elements of romance and gothic had been at the root of the evocation of the sublime. In his final letter he laments the ascendency of reason over the imagination, declaring that fancy being 'constrained against her will, to ally herself with strict truth ... what we have gotten by this is a great deal of good sense. What we have lost is a world of fine feeling.' And in letter IV we encounter his views on feudal lords, 'every lord was to be met with, like the Giant in his stronghold of a castle.' Words which, as we will see, must have lingered in Horace's mind.

Added to this, in the same year, 1762, James Macpherson had published *Fingal*, a collection of poems which he claimed were translations of a fourth century Gaelic bard called Ossian. Horace was not convinced that it was genuine, but recognised the doors it opened. Whatever the reason, the subterfuge that his was a translation of an ancient work did not stop at the title page. The Preface is a brilliant parody, not to say spoof, of academic authority and gravity.

Addressing his readers in the guise of the *translator*, Horace seeks to establish its provenance, claiming that the original had been found in the library of an ancient Catholic family in the North of England; (hence sufficiently remote) that it had been printed in Black Letter in Naples in 1529, but that the events described would suggest a date during the crusades, i.e. between 1095 and 1243. In addition to this aura of learning is the esoteric observation that the Spanish names of the domestics would tend to support the later date as it was not until the establishment of the Arragonian Kings in Naples in 1266 that 'such appellations became familiar in that country.' The dry tone and the finicky detail are absolutely convincing; this is a university man who knows what he is talking about.

Warning his readers that some of the Catholic beliefs 'savour of barbarism', and explaining that it was written 'during the darkest ages of Christianity', he turns his attention to the supposed author, a canon of the Church of St Nicholas Otranto and with the outlandish name of Onuphrio Muralto. He suggests that the aim of this 'artful priest', might have been to reaffirm 'the populace in their ancient errors and superstitions', and that the book was in fact part of the literary counter-reformation. Thus, via the persona of William Marshall, Horace appears to be excusing the fantasy and preternatural events, yet on the other hand to favour them when he regrets that they are 'exploded now even from romance.' He even manages to praise his own work: 'the characters are well drawn and still better maintained.' And again, 'However, with all its faults, I have no doubt but the English reader will be pleased with the sight of this performance.' The pretence is carried out to the extent that 'William Marshall', the supposed translator, even proposes to print the original Italian! And through him Horace wryly suggests that the story took place in a real castle and that 'Curious persons, who have leisure to employ in such researches may possibly discover ... the foundation upon which our author has built.' Horace was enjoying the game; there can be no doubt of that. But what was this story which curious people were about to read?

At the outset we are told that an ominous prophecy hangs over Otranto: 'That the Castle and Lordship of Otranto should pass from the present family whenever the real owner should be grown too large to inhabit it.' Before we even have a chance to wonder what such enigmatic words could possibly amount to, catastrophe strikes. A gigantic helmet falls, seemingly from nowhere, and crushes to death the young prince Conrad moments before his wedding. The reaction of his father, Manfred, the villain of the piece, is that this presents him with a splendid opportunity to divorce his wife and marry the lovely bride, Isabella. She, understandably, is horrified by the idea. She flees and aided by a 'peasant' escapes through secret passages under the castle to the sanctuary of a nearby church. Alonso The Good, a previous Lord of the Castle, is seen to step down from his portrait, sigh and vanish into an upper chamber, and two demented servants claim to have seen a gigantic armoured leg and foot there. Isabella meanwhile is safely in sanctuary, but Manfred still insists on his right to marry her. A friar, Jerome, in order to protect her, puts it into Manfred's mind that she is in love with the 'peasant'. Manfred, in a rage sentences the 'peasant' to death, but just as he bares his neck for the axe, the friar sees, and lo and behold, recognises a birthmark. The 'peasant' is his son, Theodore, and in fact of noble birth as the friar was once the Count of Falconara. Just then the sound of a trumpet is heard; it is a splendid cliff-hanger end to the chapter. Things then begin to get complicated ...

Readers were thrilled by it. It had opened a door onto a world which had been closed to them for so long – a world of the exotic, the strange, the supernatural and the mysterious, the dark underside of the Age of Reason. It can also be looked upon as the architectural flamboyance of Strawberry Hill recreated on the written page. It went through twelve editions during Horace's lifetime and more than a hundred after his death. It was something so startlingly new. As a genre the novel itself was comparatively new of course. For centuries there had been romances (Horace had devoured them while at Eton) celebrating the achievements and sometimes the downfall of heroes and royals, but Defoe and Fielding had begun to show their readers life as they saw it around them, while Richardson was intent on exploring their inner lives. But nothing had prepared them for *Otranto*. As they turned its pages there was no way they could guess what was going to happen next.

The initial reaction among Horace's friends was somewhat mixed however, perhaps a little puzzled, even embarrassed perhaps that someone so sophisticated could publish something so extravagantly shocking and at the same time so popular. Gilly Williams, in a letter to George Selwyn, dismissed it as 'such a novel as no boarding-school miss of 13 could get through without yawning.' And Gray's thankyou letter to Horace borders on the supercilious. 'It engages our attention here [in Cambridge] makes some of us cry a little and all in general afraid to go to bed o'night.' Gray is not a man it is easy to warm to.

But he is not really frightened. He is laughing, but his laughter is not in any way mocking. He has inadvertently put his finger on one of the curious features of the horror novel – its propensity for comedy. The relationship between fear and laughter is fascinating, as is that between happiness and tears.

'You made me jump!' someone will say and immediately laugh. And higher up the emotional scale, real terror is quite likely to be the occasion of hysterics. One of the things which attracted early cinema audiences to Hammer films was, as I myself remember, that the 'horror' was sometimes preposterous. Horror stories are a far remove from tragedies. There is no element of catharsis. We do not identify with the protagonists in any way. It is not even a case of comedy being tragedy that happens to somebody else. We know that the situations are as far removed from our own reality as it is possible to be. We know that it is not real. It is fun. We laugh at the incongruity, yet are awkwardly aware that it is perhaps something we should not be laughing at. Equally, and importantly, it could be said to be reflecting the new aesthetic of the sublime which established a link between fear and pleasure.

In *The Castle of Otranto*, Horace has immediately captured this effect. When a hooded figure turns and proves to be a skeleton, it only makes us jump, whereas in the story it was an event which would doubtless have driven Manfred out of his wits.

The literary journals swallowed the bait they were offered by the first edition and took it seriously, assuming that it was an authentic piece of medieval literature. The *Monthly* (February 1764) after some objections to the 'absurdities of Gothic fictions', concluded, 'However, as a work of genius, evincing great dramatic powers and exhibiting fine views of nature, *The Castle of Otranto* may still be read with great pleasure.' And although the *Critical Review* had some hard things to say, it too concluded that, 'excepting those absurdities, the characters are well marked and the narrative kept up with surprising spirit and propriety.'

The reaction of *Otranto's* general readers was far more simple. They were enthralled. They read on with delight to discover that the trumpet heralded the arrival of a noblemen bearing a gigantic sword and claiming to represent and champion Isabella. She escapes again with Theodore, the sometime-peasant, who savagely wounds one of their pursuers, only to find out that it is her father. Meanwhile, in the castle, things have been getting complicated again: drops of blood have been seen to fall from the nose of the statue of Alfonso; a skeleton in the robes of a monk appears and then a gigantic armoured hand on the banisters of the great stairway. Manfred, in a fit of jealous, rage stabs his daughter to death having mistaken her for Isabella. The earlier prophecy then comes to pass as the gigantic re-assembled phantom of Alphonso rises up and causes the Castle to collapse, as he cries out, 'Behold, in Theodore the true heir of Alphonso!' Theodore and Isabella marry and probably live happily ever after. Manfred is shipped off to a monastery and his wife to a convent where, presumably, they don't. This is, one might say, the skeleton of the story.

It was the second edition, however, which truly established it. Emboldened by the success of the first, Horace dropped all the pretence, acknowledged his authorship and changed the title page to read, 'The Castle of Otranto, a Gothic Story'. He also added an epigraph from the opening of the Roman poet Horace's *'Ars Poetica'* which his more learned readers would have recognised as being not quite right. By changing two small words what should have read 'a poet's fantasies are like a sick man's raving dream in which you can't tell head from foot', it has now become 'nevertheless head and foot can be assigned a single shape' – a very cunning reference to the plot line of his own story, while also arguing that while it may violate the usual conventions of literary propriety, it has a new artistic and aesthetic coherence of its own.

In 1767 he had written to Mme du Deffand 'j'ai volu qu'elle (the first edition) passât pour ancienne et presque tout le monde fut le dupe.' The literary journals, however, were not well pleased to find they had been duped, and so very publicly. The *Monthly Review* now claimed that the absurd and monstrous fictions it contained had made them suspicious from the start and turned on Horace, 'It is indeed more than strange that an author of a refined and polished genius, should be an advocate for re-establishing the barbarous superstitions of Gothic devilism!' The *Critical Review* let him down more lightly, but he was not much bothered by their reaction. Writing again to Mme du Deffand, he insisted:

> Let the critics have their say; I shall not be vexed; it was not written for this age which wants nothing but cold reason. I own to you that of all my works, it is the only one in which I pleased myself. I let my imagination run; my visions and my passions kindled me. I wrote it in defiance of rules, critics and philosophers and it seems to me all the better for that. I am convinced that in some later time when taste resumes the throne from which philosophy has pushed it, that my poor castle will find admirers; it has them even today coming on; I have just published the third edition.

The critics seem not to have paid much attention to the Preface to the second edition which is a cogent essay seeking to establish the ground rules of what was to be heralded as a new literary genre, a genre which became so popular that within a matter of decades Jane Austen could satirise it in *Northanger Abbey*.

Horace was not impressed by the novels popular at that time, and certainly not by the sentimentalism of Richardson. Remembering – and who could forget? – Johnson's assertion that anyone who read *Clarissa* for the story would hang themselves, we wonder how such readers would have reacted to finding on page 2 of *Otranto* that the bridegroom had been crushed to death by a massive helmet. Nothing would have prepared them for that as, like most of us, they would probably have skipped the Preface and gone straight for the story.

Today, however, that Preface is regarded as a literary manifesto declaring that there were two kinds of romance, the ancient and the modern. While conceding that the actions, sentiments and conventions of the old romances were often unnatural and improbable, he regrets that in the modern ones, 'the great resources of fancy have been dammed up by strict adherence to common life.' What he has sought to achieve, he says, is a blend, to reconcile the two kinds, 'leaving the powers of fancy at liberty to expatiate through the boundless realms of invention while ensuring that its characters think, speak, and act as it might be supposed mere men and women would do in extraordinary positions.' To what extent he had achieved this, he modestly declined to say, but hoped that he had, 'paved a road for men of brighter talents.' *Men,* we notice – he had not anticipated Mrs Radcliffe or Mary Shelley.

Another issue which seems to concern him keenly is the 'characters of the domestics'. In his First Preface he feared that people might find them, 'too little serious for the general cast of the story', but defends them by comparing them to the gravediggers in *Hamlet* and the Roman citizens in *Julius Caesar.* He takes issue at length with Voltaire who had argued that, 'such mixture of buffoonery and solemnity is intolerable.' It is a fundamental classic v romantic issue. Voltaire regarded Shakespeare as a primitive, uncouth genius who lacked the dramatic purity of Corneille. Although *Otranto* was published in the year following the end of the Seven Years war against France, it would seem that aesthetic wars had not ceased. Even the naturalistic landscape gardens of England were seen as being in opposition to the tyrannical regimentation of Louis XIV's Versailles.

Walpole insisted that in Shakespeare, 'the great master of Nature', he had a higher authority, and concludes, 'the result of all I have said is to shelter my own daring under the canon of the brightest genius this country has produced.' It is interesting that his comparisons are always with the theatre. He repeatedly refers to the characters in his story as 'actors'. The book is divided into five chapters or acts and each ends on a moment of genuine suspense. He notes that, 'The rules of the drama [i.e. the three unities of Time, Place and Action] are almost observed throughout the conduct of the piece' and under the guise of the 'translator' in the Preface to the First Edition he says of the 'author', 'It is a pity that he did not apply his talents to what they were evidently proper for, the theatre.'

It should not be forgotten that Horace was a keen theatre-goer throughout his life, from his first visit to Paris on his Grand Tour right up until 1793 when at the age of 76 he told Mary Berry that he 'had been twice to the play this week.' He was also an avid reader of plays and when his library was eventually dispersed in 1824 it contained copies of 550 different plays. He understood the theatre. But he was a difficult man to please and his letters show him frequently very critical of performances he had seen. However, he greatly enjoyed the company of theatre people and this at a time when for many of his contemporaries the very word *actress* carried more than a degree of social stigma with it. John

Kemble and Mrs Siddons were his frequent guests and Kitty Clive who lived at Little Strawberry Hill for the last 30 years of her life, was one of his closest friends. But he had precious little time for Garrick. 'Yes, Madam, I do think the pomp of Garrick's funeral perfectly ridiculous,' he wrote to Lady Ossory and went on at some length to accuse him of poor declamation and 'too much art.' He was, in his view, 'as vain as he was jealous', nor 'was he a real gentleman.' On this one occasion he might even have agreed with Johnson that 'Garrick has not made Shakespeare better known; he does not understand him.'

In some ways almost everything Horace says in his Prefaces can be seen as a part of the homage to Shakespeare which was growing in the eighteenth century and this again makes us alive to the dramatic qualities of the novel itself. It is strongly visual from the start when the huge helmet crushes poor Conrad to death and then when Manfred was about to pursue Isabella.

> The moon which was now up and gleamed in at the opposite casement, presented to his sight the plumes of the fatal helmet, which rose to the height of the windows, waving backwards and forwards in a tempestuous manner and accompanied with a hollow and rustling sound.

There is the shock element of Alonso the Good stepping out of his portrait, but the moment which inspired most of the illustrations is when Isabella's father sees a robed figure kneeling before an altar.

> ... the figure rising, stood some moments fixed in meditation, without regarding him. The marquis, expecting the holy person to come forth and meaning to excuse his uncivil interruption,

said 'Reverend father ... ' And then the figure turning slowly round, discovered to Frederic the fleshless jaws and empty sockets of a skeleton wrapped in a hermit's cowl.

Delaying the finale with a long, slow preamble is so well done, as are the cliff-hanger endings to the chapters/acts.

His characters may have few of the shades of personality we meet with in Richardson and Fielding; they are mostly reduced to the simplest terms: wicked, valiant, chaste etc. yet apart from the (deliberately?) overblown romantic protestations of Theodore, the dialogue is convincing and makes up a great part of the novel. All his characters sound like distinctive individuals and that is equally true of the domestics and especially so of the garrulous Bianca, who is given some splendid malapropisms and is genuinely funny.

There are also several direct and indirect quotations from Shakespeare, as, when echoing the appearance of Hamlet's ghost, Jerome says to his son, ' ... list, while a father unfolds a tale of horror that will expel every sentiment from your soul, but sentiments of sacred vengeance.'

The oddest dramatic feature, however, is the introduction in Chapter 3 of what amount to stage directions in square brackets. 'There, take my gage [Giving him his ring]' And again 'Pardon these tears! [The knights gazed at each other, wondering where this would end.]' A literary device which no other novelist followed up.

Horace had come across a note in Warburton's edition of Pope's *Collected Works* which referred to *Otranto*, declaring it to be, 'regularly a drama', but dismissed it as an 'intention I am sure I do not pretend to have conceived.' This was in a letter to

Richard Jephson who had written a play *The Count of Narbonne* based on the novel. Horace himself had been involved not only in the writing of the play but had attended almost all the rehearsals and was here congratulating Jephson on the production which had been staged at Covent Garden in November 1781. Jephson had cut out all the comedy and, not surprisingly, had been unable to portray the falling of the helmet or the Poe-like collapse of the castle. Nevertheless, Horace was pleased with what he had done. 'I must again applaud your art and judgment, Sir, in having made so rational a play out of my wild tale.' It was a theatrical success, performed 21 times and regularly produced over the next two decades.

Horace continued to make light of his achievement, telling Mann, 'It is not everybody in this country that may play the fool with impunity.' But it was not long before his work was being taken seriously, and especially by Sir Walter Scott, who would come to be recognised as the master of historical romance and who acknowledged the influence of Walpole in the preface to his first novel *Waverley*. Dismissing the once popular French romances as, 'the dullest of dull folios', he praises Horace for being the first modern to found a tale of amusing fiction upon the basics of the ancient romances of Chivalry and for having rescued the very term *Gothic* from 'the bad fame into which it had fallen.'

In a delightful sentence Scott recognises Horace's achievement as an antiquary: 'He brings with him the torch of genius to illuminate the ruins through which he loves to wander.' At the same time, he recognises his ability to demonstrate, 'that accurate exhibition of human characteristics and contrasts of feelings and passions, which is, or ought to be, delineated in the modern novel.' He finds the characters strongly drawn and praises the purity of the language. His one reservation is that there is perhaps too much supernatural interference, but 'it is more than compensated by the high merit of the many and marvellous incidents in the romance.'

There are marvellous incidents in this first 'Gothic story' which seem equally to be harbingers of surrealism. It is an element which, at first sight, would appear to have sprung out of nowhere, but its origins become clear when we think again of Horace's claim in the Second Preface, 'that the great resources of fancy have been dammed up by strict adherence to common life', for the reverse is equally true. When life is in a state of flux, danger and uncertainty, it may well be then that the imagination craves order. As Auden wrote in his essay on Tennyson, 'It will may be, I think, that the more he [the poet] is conscious of an inner disorder and dread, the more value he will place on tidiness "in the work".' And in an age that had grown too fond of Reason and was starved of action, the imagination began to dream of violence, and subconscious fears and desires were seen to rise up. In the *Castle of Otranto* no one is safe; there is no refuge anywhere. But the threat is even greater in the play which Horace wrote in 1768, *The Mysterious Mother*.

The storyline of this play is as complex, but more compact than *The Castle of Otranto*. Again the action takes place at Narbonne and in the early years of the Reformation. Sixteen years previously, we are told, the Countess of Narbonne had been awaiting the return of the Count her husband who had been away at war for a year and a half, but just as he was nearing the castle he was killed by a ferocious stag. It is made clear that the Countess, a passionate woman, had been eagerly anticipating their sexual reunion. Learning that her son, Edmund, was planning an assignation with her maid, Beatrice, that very night, she took the girl's place, intending to confront and rebuke him. However, the son being the image of his father, her frustrated passion overcame her. As a result, a daughter, Adeliza, is born. She is brought up in a nearby convent as an orphan and Edmund is banished. But after sixteen years he returns with his friend Florian, encounters Adeliza and falls in love with her. A 'meddling' friar, Benedict, outraged by the Countess's Protestant leanings and eventually suspecting her 'fatal secret', deceives her into agreeing to a marriage between the two young people. (She had believed Florian was to be the groom.) Thus, Adeliza is now Edmund's daughter, sister and wife! Learning the truth of this, the Countess kills herself, Adeliza returned to the convent and Edmund goes back to war and to 'rush on death'.

The 'bed-trick', as it is called, was a traditional folktale device. It features in Shakespeare's *All's Well that Ends Well*. Nor were the events resulting from the incestuous union Horace's own invention, as he pointed out in a Postscript to the edition of 1781. He had heard, he says, that a gentlewoman had confessed the same story to Archbishop Tillotson (presumably in the 1690's) and sought his advice. 'The prelate charged her never to let her son and daughter know what had passed as they were innocent of any criminal intention. For herself, he bade her almost despair.' Nevertheless, not everyone was prepared to forgive Horace for having made dramatic use of something quite so *horrid*. In a letter to George Montagu, he claimed that, 'Mr Chute, who is not easily pleased, likes it, and Gray, who is still more difficult, approves of it', but did admit that he was 'not yet intoxicated enough with it to think it would do for the stage, though I wish to see it acted.' Perhaps he saw it as a 'closet drama' and told Montagu that some friends would soon be coming to Strawberry Hill to read through it together. There was another such reading in November 1786 at Windsor Palace, but it was an evening which did not go well, as Fanny Burney records in her journal, 'Dreadful was the whole! truly dreadful! a story of so much horror, of atrocious & voluntary guilt, never did I hear! ... For myself, I felt a sort of indignant aversion rise fast & warm in my mind against the wilful Author of a story so horrible ... which made me regard him as the patron of the vices he had been pleased to record.'

Coleridge went even further. ' ... the most disgusting, detestable, vile composition that ever came from the hand of man.' Adding an unnecessary homophobic slur: 'No one with a spark of true manliness, of which Walpole had none, could have written it.'

Horace must have been spending 'a quiet Christmas' at Strawberry Hill in 1767, as it was then that work on the play had begun. At first it went well; he was writing quickly and fluently, but having completed the first three acts he put it to one side. Why we do not know, but for the next fifteen months he was occupied with political matters; spent some time in Paris and wrote *Historic Doubts on the Life and Reign of Richard III* which was published on 1st February 1768. But he resumed work on it and by April of the same year he had finished the last two acts, and though he was not totally happy with them, *The Mysterious Mother* appeared under the Strawberry Hill imprint, in a small octavo edition limited to 50 copies, most of which went as gifts to friends.

It was perhaps this blend of scarcity and scandal which quickly drew to it something of a mystique. In the opening of his article in the *Monthly Review* of July 1797 William Taylor refers to it as, 'this far-famed tragedy'. And goes on, 'We seize the opportunity of noticing it; for there is a pleasure in announcing one of those works of art to which genius has affixed the stamp of immortality.' That does seem to be rather extreme, but it is an interesting point he makes when comparing it with Sophocles' *Oedipus*: 'The English author has indeed exchanged the trim simplicity of action which was habitual to the Greek stage, for the artful complexity of intrigue that is expected on our own.' And it is interesting that in his *Biographica Dramatica* of 1782, Isaac Reed admits that to stage the play, 'would be extremely hazardous ... but we cannot but observe at the same time, that the delicacy of the present times is frequently carried to a ridiculous degree of affectation.' Horace would have agreed with him, ' ... at least it does not resemble this century's prim and conventional tone,' he suggested to Mme du Deffand. But the praise Reed heaped on it was nothing to equal that of Byron – no friend to squeamish delicacy and happy to defend a fellow nobleman.

> It is the fashion to underrate Horace Walpole; firstly because he was a nobleman, and secondly because he was a gentleman; but to say nothing of the composition of his incomparable letters, and of *The Castle of Otranto,* he is the 'Ulitmus Romanorum, the author of *Mysterious Mother*, a tragedy of the highest order, and not a puling love-play. He is the father of the first romance, and of the last tragedy in our language, and surely worthy of a higher place than any living writer, be he who he may.

The Mysterious Mother, A Tragedy is how the title page reads. We all know, or think that we know, what a tragedy *is*, but it is a difficult concept to come to grips with in its entirety. The idea of a 'tragic flaw' in the nature of the tragic hero seems to accept the challenging proposition that an audience will be able to psychoanalyse a character while watching things happen on stage. More plausible, I think, is to expect the tragic events to occur as the result of what is seen to be *happening*: some event; some action. What has been called 'The Crime Against Love' seems to me to be at the root of so many of the most outstanding tragedies. It is epitomised in Othello's protestation to Desdemona in one of his happier moments.

> Excellent wretch! Perdition catch my soul
> But I do love thee! And when I love thee not,
> Chaos is come again.

And chaos is assuredly what does come when he is 'led by the nose' into a fit of murderous jealousy. In the term, 'The Crime Against Love', *love* need not be seen as restricted solely to *amour*, to affairs of the heart. The opposite of chaos is *order* and divine love is what created order out of chaos. The *Crime* may therefore be seen as being equally against other aspects of *love*, including political and civil order, as it most assuredly is *King Lear*. When he rejects his youngest daughter's love, Lear's words 'Nothing will come of nothing' are more prophetic than he realises. And the chaos that can be brought about in a marriage by false accusation is painfully evident in *The Winter's Tale*.

The Countess of Narbonne certainly commits a crime against love, and so is, unusually, a female tragic hero. This may initially seem an unlikely proposition, unless we come to it, as of course we should any play, by pretending that we do not know how it ends. And as Horace claimed in a letter to Richard Jephson, 'If there is any merit in my play, I think it is in interrupting the spectator's fathoming the whole story till the last.' Approaching it, therefore, as it were for the first time means that we need to concentrate our attention on what we *see* and what we are *told* at the very beginning.

The Prologue, which was not printed until the 1798 edition of *The Works*, opens with a dismissal of the Classical Principles as they persisted in French drama.

> From no French model breathes the Muse to-night,
> The scene she draws is horrid, not polite.

Instead, he tells us, his models will be 'Shakespeare's magic' and 'the nobler licence of the Greeks.' This will not in any way blunt the play's moral purpose. 'Can crimes be punish'd by a bard enchain'd?' he asks. And just as, for the Greeks, 'Whatever passion prompted was their game', so his story, 'though not nice', as he admits, 'from real life it rose,' and will, he hopes, ultimately evoke both terror and pity.

At the outset there is no hint of terror, but plenty to arouse our pity. Who would not feel pity for a lady whose husband, returning to her from eighteen months away at war, meets a violent accidental death when almost home? And who, on finding out that her son, instead of mourning for his father, was planning a sexual liaison with one of her maids that same night, would not have sent him packing? Nevertheless, this 'pious countess' still prays for him daily. It is her piety that is stressed in this opening dialogue between the young count's friend Florian and old Peter the Porter: as are her prayers, her fasting and her charity to the poor. And in our first view of her, as she silently crosses the stage, she is dressed in widow's weeds and holding a crucifix.

The first word of criticism against her comes in the following scene between two friars, Martin and Benedict, but proves to be yet another mark in her favour, as what they object to is her leaning towards Protestantism. Anti-Catholic sentiments are, as we will see, heavily stressed throughout the play and Horace puts words enough into their own mouths to damn them. 'Win power by craft; wear it with ostentation.'

'Meddling monks' were to become a standard feature of Gothic fiction, yet Horace's attitude to Catholicism is ever-ambiguous. From the early years of his Grand Tour the aesthetics of it had fascinated him: the gorgeous vestments, the frescoes and the music, the smells and bells. And in his own account of the Strawberry Hill Chapel we read of 'a crucifix of bronze; and beneath it an angular pedestal of faience on which is a bust of an angel, stands an encensoir of bronze. By the door is a holy-water-pot of earthenware.' The trappings were, it would seem, things he could hardly get enough of, but the Papacy itself – NO. We recall Andrew Marvell's comment, 'Popery is such a thing as cannot be called a Religion.' The Papacy, as far as Horace was concerned, was political and smacked of all things Tory and Jacobite; the uprising of 1745 still being recent enough to bring back bitter memories.

The first act ends with an angry encounter between the Countess and the friars in which she vehemently rejects what she sees as the hypocrisy of their concern, yet such is Horace's skill that the first faint suspicions about her begin to be aroused. If she so assiduously avoids confession, is there not something she is afraid to confess?

Our sympathies remain with her however and when we first encounter the young Count Edmund he does little to endear himself to us. He seems to see nothing wrong in having sex with one of the maids shortly after the death of his father. Indeed he challenges his friend:

> Wouldst thou have turned thee from a willing girl,
> To sing a requiem to thy father's soul?

That's one way of putting it. But he is entitled to be puzzled as to why he should be banished, while his mother still allows him the revenue of his estates and in her letters sends her blessings. 'I must know this riddle,' he says. And so, we begin to feel, must we. Another reason he is determined to stay in Narbonne is that he has fallen in love – these things happen – with 'young Adeliza.'

Unlike, let us say, T.S. Eliot, Horace Walpole was aware that a drama needs something more than people talking to each other. Something needs to happen and that *Something* in this case is a procession of orphans singing a hymn with the ominous final lines:

> Cloath the penitent with grace;
> And guilt's foul spots efface! efface!

They are on their way to offer up prayers at a Cross raised in memory of the dead Count, but almost immediately they come rushing back crying in terror as the Cross has been struck by lightning and 'shiver'd to splinters.' An event which startles Martin.

> Sixteen fatal years
> Has Narbonne's province groan'd beneath the hand
> Of desolation – for what crimes we know not.

Act III develops quickly, opening with a soliloquy by the Countess. Reflecting on the meaning of these events she provides us with almost enough to explain 'the riddle'. She is then joined by Adeliza who has her own confession to make. She has allowed some 'young knight' to speak to her of love. The Countess, mistakenly believing it to be Florian, reassures her. But in a drama of this sort one mistaken identity is rarely enough. Benedict introduces a 'soldier' to the Countess, who, he expects, will confirm the death of her son, Edmund. The 'soldier' is of course Edmund himself and with a cry of 'Horror on horror!' the Countess collapses.

At this point Horace put the manuscript to one side for over a year and concentrated on his research into the life of Richard III. It is not difficult to see why he chose to have a break. He had a problem. All the characters were assembled and the situation was becoming clear. But he had two more acts to fill. How? When he took up his pen again, the way to go forward had become clear, but he seems to have lost the initial impulse and his last two acts lack the élan of the first three. It is, however, far from being as clumsy as Horace once claimed to Mme du Deffand 'From the first act until the last scene interest languishes instead of increasing; can there be a worse flaw?'

Act IV opens with another animated, if rather extended

discussion between the friars. Benedict, with an almost Iago-like malignity, declares his intention:

> I cannot dupe, and therefore must destroy her;
> Involve her house in ruin so prodigious.
> That neither she nor Edmund may survive it.

He would seem to be very close to the truth, but still claims it is her heresy she should be punished for; while proclaiming the supremacy of their faith, their cynicism and hypocrisy is made evident, even to the extent of stating:

> The church is but a specious name for empire
> And will exist wherever fools have fears.

Another procession enters, this time of friars chanting a funeral anthem. The Abbess is dead and being mourned by Adeliza. It is a diversion which does little to advance the plot, but allows the Countess, again at length, to urge Adeliza to marry and to leave Narbonne. She still believes that Florian is the girl's lover and her intention is to ensure that Adeliza and Edmund are kept as far apart as possible. But it is not to be. Adeliza and Edmund are married and by Benedict and they then present themselves to the Countess. 'Dear parent, look on us,' Edmund says in all innocence, 'and bless your children.' And with that Chaos is come again. The Countess declares herself, 'thy mother! mistress!/The mother of thy daughter, sister, wife!' And then in lines which have such power and sweep to them she leaves Edmund in no doubt.

> Yes, thou polluted son!
> Grief, disappointment, opportunity,

> Rais'd such a tumult in my madding blood,
> I took the damsel's place; and while thy arms
> Twin'd to thy thinking, round another's waist,
> Hear, hell, and tremble! – thou didst clasp thy mother!
>
> *Adeliza faints; Edmund draws his dagger to kill his mother, but she seizes it from him and kills herself.*

Edmund too longs for death, but on the battlefield.

> O Florian, we must haste,
> To where fell war assumes its ugliest form;
> I burn to rush on death.

That little word 'fell' inevitably, and deliberately, reminds us of Hamlet's 'this fell sergeant death', but beyond this there is more than a touch of that play's ending, when we realise that Fortinbras, that unlovely personage is the last man standing, and his grim order, 'Go, bid the soldiers shoot', sends us shuffling silently from the theatre, thinking to ourselves, 'Yes, that's the way things are, but I wish they weren't.' But at the close of the *Mysterious Mother* we are not given time to reflect. There is that odd, even if ancient, convention of the Epilogue. Pity and terror are blown away as Horace's actress friend Kitty Clive, a leading comedienne, takes centre stage and in bouncing, robust couplets asserts:

> I vow'd by all the gods of Rome and Greece,
> 'Twas I would finish his too doleful piece.
> I, flush'd with comic roguery – said I
> Will make 'em laugh, more than you make 'em cry.

Her tone is such fun – some outrageous rhymes – and so very

different from the five acts of blank verse which have gone before that we realise what an extraordinarily efficient poet Horace could be. His characters have each their own distinctive voice and they *talk* to each other. He can handle long paragraphs of verse as well as pack power into a single line.

> Monks may reach heav'n, but never came from thence.

And he was surely entitled to feel pleased with himself when he re-read Florian's lines:

> Pleasure has charms; but so has virtue too.
> One skims the surface, like the swallow's wing,
> And scuds away unnotic'd, 'Tother nymph
> Like spotless swans in solemn majesty,
> Breasts the full surge and leaves long light behind.

When he denied to one of his correspondents that he was ever a poet, Horace was quite wrong. Conversely, in the Preface to the first edition of The *Castle of Otranto* he was quite right when he said of its author, 'It is a pity that he did not apply his talents to what they were evidently proper for, the theatre.' And perhaps Byron knew what he was talking about when he called *The Mysterious Mother* 'a tragedy of the highest order.'

This was not his last experiment with the theatre or with fantasy. Eleven years later saw the performance, at The Little Theatre in the Haymarket, of his one–act play *Nature Will Prevail*. It features two men shipwrecked on a desert island. One by the name of *Current* never stops talking. The other, *Padlock*, is 'a morose creature' who rarely speaks. Its sub-title is 'A Moral Entertainment' and what it shows is that two people left alone, instead of collaborating for their mutual benefit, will seek to deceive, outwit and get the better of each other, especially when they discover that there is also a pretty and innocent country girl on their island. And in case the audience do not realise the 'moral' from what they see and hear, a Fairy, who has set it all up, finally declares in lines which call to mind Shakespeare's Prospero:

> I caused you all three to be transported hither to make experiment. What has been the result? You, Padlock, on an uninhabited island, have not been able to divest yourself of caution, reserve, suspicion, cunning, self-interest and treachery. one man alone was your companion; and yet you could not bring yourself to trust him; the first woman you saw, tempted you to betray him ... You, Current, are more fool than knave; but you too are incorrigible. The threats of death, the loss of hearing, could not cure you of your loquacity.

So much for the 'moral', and yet loquacity does not here seem to be such a dreadful sin.

The 'Entertainment', if one can call it that, centres mostly on Current having been rendered deaf and Padlock trying to convince him that he is also dumb; the confusion thus caused, if skilfully acted, could possibly be mildly funny. Horace's essay 'Thoughts on Comedy' is evidence that he had read widely and thought much about the topic, but knowing what is entailed in comedy and putting it into practice is a different matter. All in all, *Nature Will Prevail* is a slight and trivial piece, and yet we are told that when performed it met with some success. Nothing is odder than another age's sense of humour.

10

THE ESSAYIST

Robert Dodsley, perceptive and enterprising as ever, seems to have sensed that the grave moral tones of Johnson's *Rambler* essays were beginning to lose their appeal, and early in 1753 he launched a new periodical, *The World,* in direct opposition. Aimed at a younger readership, the world of fashion, the *beau monde,* its intention from the start was to amuse and entertain. Several of its contributors were in fact themselves members of that *beau monde,* and, interestingly, it was in *The World* that Lord Chesterfield published his whimsical piece on Johnson's *Dictionary,* and which prompted the Doctor's famous and furious reply.

Walpole's name was among the first to appear in its pages and the nine essays he wrote deserve to be better known, equalling, as they do, Chesterfield's in their elegance, learning and wit; the variety of topics he covered being a great part of their delight. In his first contribution he begins by making gentle fun of the 'new naturalism' of the theatre – a 'real' waterfall on stage. He then considers the 'new naturalism' in gardens which had even led to the planting of dead trees and the building of molehills. From there he jumps to fashionable desserts, where 'cottages rose in sugar, temples in barley-sugar; pigmy Neptunes in cars of cockle-shells triumphed over oceans of looking-glass.' One dinner party, he tells us, even ended with 'a representation of Mount Etna which vomited out real fireworks over the heads of the company.'

In his third paper he 'learnedly' takes issue with the change to the Gregorian calendar which had been imposed the previous year. That it had changed the actual days on which Saints were celebrated had upset many people and Horace adds to their argument by pointing out that pranks played by people on the *new* April Fool's Day would no longer be effective and that the Glastonbury Thorn had not been fooled as to what was the *real* Christmas Day.

Perhaps the most delightful of all his arguments is that put forward in Paper XXVIII, where he declares that, 'young women are *not* the proper objects of sensual love; it is the Matron, the Hoary Fair, who can give, communicate, insure happiness.' One of his proofs being that 'unless there were implanted in our natures a strong temptation towards the love of Elderly Women, why should the very first prohibition in the table of consanguinity forbid a man to marry his Grand Mother?' True to his word, throughout the whole of his celibate life Horace did indeed count among his closest friends several 'ladies in the bloom of their wrinkles', notably, of course, Mme du Deffand.

And this is not the only autobiographical element in these essays. In his encomium on the politeness of his native country he relates that an acquaintance of his had been robbed by a highwayman, but that 'the whole affair was conducted with the greatest good breeding.' As indeed he knew to have been the case, he himself having been the victim when held up in Hyde Park by that celebrated highwayman, James Maclean. A pistol had gone off, seemingly accidentally, the ball narrowly missing Horace and going through the roof of his coach. Maclean had then ridden away with Horace's purse, his watch and his sword together with some silver belonging to the coachman. Horace advertised in the newspapers, offering twenty guineas for the return of his property and received the following courteous reply.

> Sir, Seeing an advertisement in the papers of to Day giving an account of your being Rob'd by two highwayman on wednesday night last in Hyde Parke and during the time a Pistol being fired whether Intended or Accidentally was Doubtfull obliges us to take this Method of assuring you that it was the latter and by no means Design'd Either to hurt or frighten you for tho' we are Reduced by the misfortunes of the world and obliged to have Recourse to this method of getting money Yet we have Humanity Enough not to take any body's Life where there is Not a Necessity for it.

Could such a situation ever have been handled in a more gentlemanly way?

A meeting was arranged and a deal was done. Maclean had first asked for forty guineas, but settled for twenty. Shortly after this honourable incident, however, he was caught robbing the Salisbury coach. His trial was short and he was sentenced to be hanged at Tyburn, but not before thousands, so it is said, had visited him in his jail, many of them being society ladies weeping copiously over the fate of this handsome, romantic rogue. Horace did not witness his execution, but neither was he willing to give evidence against him. What gentleman would?

There is throughout these essays a sparkling display of learning – allusions, anecdotes, quotations – but brought to us always with the lightest of touches and self-deprecation. 'I own,' he even tells us at one point, 'if there is any species of writing of which I am not perfect master, it is the epistolary.' And this from a man whose collected correspondence runs to over 4,000 letters.

It was a letter published by him in 1757 – the year after the closure of *The World* – which so attracted pubic attention that it went through five editions in a fortnight. Its full title was, 'A Letter from Xo Ho, a Chinese philosopher at London, to his friend Lien Chi, at Peking.' In tones of Oriental gravity and Oriental bewilderment Xo Ho [pronounced, laughingly, Hoho] tries to explain to his friend the oddities of English political life at that time. It would necessitate a blizzard of footnotes to allow us today to follow the complex inadequacies it exposes, but one fact does stand out and that is the reference to Admiral Byng.

It was in 1756, in the early stages of the Seven Years' War, that the British garrison on the island of Minorca had come under siege from the French. A fleet commanded by Admiral Byng engaged them in an inconclusive skirmish, during which two of his vessels were damaged. After consulting his other captains he returned to Gibraltar which he was also under orders to defend, thus leaving Minorca to fall to the French. The humiliation of this led to a feeling of national outrage and all the blame for it fell on Byng. Mobs were heard shouting, 'Swing, swing, Admiral Byng.' In truth, years of peace and subsequent neglect and underspending by the Admiralty had meant that the fleet was undermanned and in a dangerous state of repair when it left England, but the Admiralty was never going to admit to that.

Byng was ordered home, tried by court martial and found guilty, not of cowardice, but of neglect of duty, which, nevertheless, under The Articles of War, still carried the death penalty. The injustice was blatant and several of the naval officers conducting the court martial had only agreed to the guilty verdict on the clear understanding that the sentence would not be carried out; that he would be granted mercy. Pleas were made on his behalf, but the King was unmoved and on 14 March 1757, during a howling gale, Byng was executed by a firing squad of marines on the quarter deck of HMS *Monarch* in Portsmouth harbour. He was most certainly a scapegoat and died, as Voltaire famously put it, 'pour encourager les autres', which proved to be quite true, as after him other leaders, such as Wolfe, decided they could not take such risks.

The ministers, Hardwicke, Newcastle and Fox, who had sent Byng out so ill-prepared and ill-equipped remained in their posts, and as Xo Ho put it,

> An enquiry or trial of the late ministers was determined: the imprisoned admiral was tried, acquitted, condemned and put to death. The trial of the others were delayed. At last they were tried – not as I expected, whether they were guilty, but whether they should be ministers again or not. If the executed Admiral had lived, he too might have been a minister.

Walpole was sickened and disgusted by the events, declaring that Byng was, 'marked for sacrifice by a set of ministers, who meant to divert on him the vengeance of a betrayed and enraged nation.' Hampered by not being an MP at that time, he did all he could to win him a reprieve and though he managed to secure a brief stay of execution, his ultimate failure only saddened him the more. Writing to Mann, he admitted ' ... to my infinite grief, which I shall feel till the man is at peace, I have been instrumental in protracting his misery a fortnight, by what I meant as the kindest thing I could do.'

It could be said that he was politically motivated by his aversion to Newcastle who had been behind his father's downfall and his opposition to the excess of royal power, but his letters show his concern to have been totally for the man, and a man he hardly knew.

His pamphlet could have got him into serious trouble. Kitty Clive exclaimed, 'Lord! You'll be sent to the Tower.' To which he replied, 'Well, my father was there before me.'

One of the few honourable things to come out of this rather grubby series of events is the inscription on Admiral Byng's monument at Southill in Bedfordshire:

> To the Perpetual Disgrace of Public Justice
> The Honourable John Byng, Esqre
> Admiral of the Fleet
> Fell a Martyr to Political Persecution
> March 14th in the Year 1757, when
> Bravery and Loyalty
> Were Insufficient Securities for the
> Life and Honour
> Of a Naval Officer

There is one observation early in Xo Ho's letter which chimes in so closely with 21st century politics that it cries out to be recorded:

Here one is told something every day; the people demand to be told something, no matter what: if a politician, a minister, a member of their assembly, was mysterious and refused to impart something to an enquirer, he would make an enemy; if he tells a lie, it is no offence; he is communicative; that is sufficient to a *free* people; all they ask is news; a falsehood is as much news as truth.

***

One thing about Horace Walpole of which we can be quite sure is that even his closest friends could rarely have guessed what he was going to do next. Could Gray, in Ravenna, have foreseen Strawberry Hill? We know from his letters that the Strawberry Hill Press, which was soon to publish his own Odes, came as an equal shock to him. So in 1768 the publication of 'Historic Doubts on the Life and Reign of King Richard III' must have taken everyone by surprise, especially those few friends who knew that the same year had seen the appearance of 'The Mysterious Mother'. It was in fact this book on Richard which he was writing during the break he had taken between Acts Three and Four of that grisly play. Melodrama, history, melodrama – it makes for an odd sandwich.

Some monarchs do tend to stand out from the rest, surrounded as they are by an aura of myth and legend. Henry VIII by reason of his sheer bulk and six wives. Elizabeth I, Gloriana, the Virgin Queen, forever robed in the splendour of her majesty. But close to the top of the list comes Richard III, that epitome of evil, the limping, hunchbacked psychopath. Myths of him might perhaps have been carried a little too far; he was probably not, as some claimed, in his poor mother's womb for two years, only to pop out with a full set of teeth and hair down to his waist.

But Richard III has always attracted attention. There has been an active, and international, Richard III Society since 1924, and it was they who in 2012 instigated the excavation of a car park in Leicester, and the discovery there of his mutilated remains. It was a discovery which promptly caught public interest and huge crowds, including members of the royal family, attended his re-interment in the cathedral where white roses were in abundance and where there is now a Richard III Visitors Centre.

What attracted Horace might well have been David Garrick's portrayal of the character. It was in October 1741 in an unlicensed London theatre, Goodman's Fields, that the young actor so astonished his audience that he became almost instantly a celebrity. Four years later, Hogarth painted the famous portrait of him as Richard in his tent, terrified by nightmares on the eve of the Battle of Bosworth. It was a part Garrick played many times and it can be safely assumed that Horace saw it. He did tell Lady Ossory that he thought the pomp attending Carrick's funeral was rather excessive for a player (there were 34 coaches carrying the mourners) but conceded that he was 'a real genius in his way, and who, I believe, was never equalled in both tragedy and comedy.'

There can be little doubt that it is Shakespeare's view of Richard which has had a lasting and devastating influence on public opinion. As Edward Gibbon put it, 'The crimes of Richard represented in our theatres for a century and a half have become established in the minds of all with an authority that history alone could not have given them.' In the opening lines of the play

Shakespeare has him tell us, 'I am determined to prove a villain.' And insults are quickly piled on him by others, 'minister of hell', and 'lump of foul deformity'. But what always needs to be kept in mind is that the play was first performed around the year 1592, during the reign of Elizabeth I, who was descended from the usurper Henry VII, and so it can be viewed as a most successful piece of Tudor propaganda.

While there were many eager to disparage Richard, there were others ready to defend him and the argument had begun almost as soon as he was dead. John Rous in a history of the Warwick family had called him 'a good lord', but quickly re-wrote that passage when he realised which side had won the civil war.

Horace had read widely and deeply into most of what had been written about Richard, but opened his Preface by challengingly calling into question the ability and even the integrity of the 'generality of historians', not, as it later proved, a gambit which was likely to gain him many friends among those academics who had already entered the field. Among a more generalised readership, however, the book was an instant success. An edition of 1250 copies, priced at 5/- each, was published on 1 February 1768, and by the following day there was not a copy to be had and a further thousand had to be rushed into print, suggesting that after *Otranto*, Horace was now a well-known and popular author with a keen following.

If the opening of the Preface looks challenging, what follows is thumpingly assertive, ' ... it is almost a question whether, if the dead of past ages could revive, they would be able to reconnoitre the events of their own times, as transmitted to us by ignorance and misrepresentation.' And he is in no doubt who was responsible for such misrepresentation – the Roman Catholic Church: 'Swarms of foreign monks were turned loose upon us to bewilder and confound the plain good sense of our ancestors.' And 'the confusions which attended the civil war between the houses of York and Lancaster threw an obscurity over that part of our annals which it is almost impossible to dispel.' Concluding, he claims, 'If I do not flatter myself, I have unravelled a considerable part of that dark period.'

The stance he proposes to adopt is an interesting one and could be described as a logical neutrality, for whereas he is quite prepared to admit that Richard might well have been as evil as many claim him to have been, the evidence we have is not such as would prove him to have been so.

It is that very evidence which he says he will examine and when he outlines his aims one cannot but admire the degree of their objectivity.

> I will state the list of crimes charged on Richard; I will specify the authorities on which he was accused; I will give a faithful account of the historians by whom he was accused; and will then examine the circumstances of each crime and each evidence; and lastly, show that some of the crimes were contrary to Richard's interest, and almost all inconsistent with probability or with dates, and some of them involved in material contradictions.

He lists the seven alleged crimes which he will consider, beginning with 'The murder of Edward Prince of Wales, son of Henry VI', then gathers together the evidence put forward by various authorities and historians, starting with the 15th century *Chronicles of Croyland* in which no one is specifically named as the murderer, and then the account of Thomas Fabian who blamed it on 'the King's servants'. A later writer, Edmund Hall, implicates Clarence as well as both Gloucester and the Marquis of Dorset. After this he shows that Holinshed simply echoes Hall and John Stowe follows Fabian. None of this, he says, provides sufficient grounds, and as Richard had nothing to gain by such a murder, 'this crime was therefore so unnecessary, and is so far from being established by any authority that he deserves to be entirely acquitted of it.' One would tend to agree, even if Horace's bias does show when he argues that, 'some have swallowed implicitly all the vulgar tales propagated by the Lancastrians to blacken the House of York.'

Similarly and equally perfunctorily, Richard is then cleared of any implication in the deaths of Henry VI or of his brother George Duke of Clarence. The next issue is, however, more complex: the case of his nephews, the Princes in the Tower. The Tower has such a blood-stained reputation that even in the 18th century Horace needed to remind his readers that in Richard's day it was a royal palace and that it was traditional for monarchs, including Elizabeth I, to spend the night before their coronation there. This certainly alters our preconceptions.

Firstly, Horace disputes at some length the arguments put forward by Sir Thomas More in 1514 to deny Richard's entitlement to the throne. At that date More was a rising public servant under Henry VIII and so had a vested interest in blackening Richard and enhancing the Tudor line, which could be said to be quite as much a usurpation as they insisted Richard's was. Surprisingly, some of the extracts quoted from More's 'History of King Richard III' are said to be verbatim conversations which he claimed took place and make the book seem rather more of a novella than a history. As Horace puts it, 'a work of fiction and romance.'

Horace then goes on to show that Richard had convinced parliament and the people of the illegitimacy of Edward's children, and therefore of his own clear right to the throne which he had then been 'invited' to ascend. Once crowned he would have had had nothing to fear from the illegitimate Princes and even if he had decided that the best way to secure his position was to have them killed, he would have needed it to be *known* that they were dead, but no such announcement was made and even Thomas More admitted that 'the deaths and final fortunes of the two young princes have nevertheless so far come into question that some remained long in doubt, whether they were in his days destroyed or no.' Likewise Bacon confirms that there were 'secret rumours that the two young sons were not indeed murdered, but conveyed secretly away and were yet living.' It was more than a decade after their supposed deaths that Henry VII declared that they had been murdered by Richard, and that being when the appearance of the claimants Lambert Simnel and Perkin Warbeck made it essential that the princes were known to have been long dead and at the hands of his villainous predecessor.

But recounting and re-arguing historical events is best left in the hands of historians. Rather more to our purpose is the context – the medium rather than the message. And it becomes increasingly irritating to keep coming across that word *dilettante*, even on the cover of W.H. Hammond's authoritative edition of the 'Historic Doubts'. ' He cites Horace's 'dilettante style' adding that 'he was not a scholar' and lacked 'source materials'. In fact it is clear that he had not only carefully read all the available secondary sources (Croyland, Fabian, Hall, Holinshed, More, Bacon, and Polydore Vergil) he had also discovered among the Harleian MSS in the British Museum a letter from Richard to his mother, and was also able to correct 'another of Sir T. More's errors, for in the public acts is a deed of Edward the Fourth dated June 17th.'

What he had thought was his major discovery, however, was an entry in the Coronation Roll, 'To the Lord Edward son of the late Edward the Fourth, for his apparel and array ... ' The long list of gowns and fabrics which followed he took to be evidence that the young prince was not only alive but present at his uncle's coronation ceremony. That he was proved to be very much mistaken on this score does not invalidate his scholarly investigation of the source materials.

His 'Historic Doubts' is a thoroughly professional piece of work – reasoned, logical, and so carefully organised that it is doubtful if a trained lawyer could have done better. Indeed Voltaire – and we have to remember that Horace had been bitingly critical of him in the Preface to 'Otranto' – wrote, 'You would be an excellent attorney general.'

Initially, reviewers were generous in their praise, but soon the professional antiquarians, perhaps feeling that their bailiwick was being intruded upon, became hostile and some of the hostility was personal. Particularly critical were papers read at meetings of the Society of Antiquaries, and especially one by the President, Jeremiah Milles which completely overturned Horace's 'discovery' in the Coronation Rolls. Another member, Robert Masters pointed out additional errors and in a way which clearly upset Horace, being almost contemptuous. He felt that he at least warranted their respect. In a letter to lord Dacre in March 1777 he referred to them as, 'childish or rather womanish replies to my book.' He wrote three closely argued responses, but did not publish them though they were included in his *Works* of 1798. Perhaps he was too proud to wish to be involved in public controversy. As he told Mason, 'My answers shall sometime or other appear when I only shall be blamed and my antagonists will be dead and not hurt by me.'

He made his feelings clear, however, by resigning from the Society, but so as not to look piqued gave as his reason that the Society had made itself look ridiculous, as indeed it had, by investigating the history of Dick Whittington and his cat.

***

In 1785 Horace published, under the Strawberry Hill imprint, a collection of six short stories with the title of *Hieroglyphic Tales*. In his Preface he claims that he will be printing a hundred thousand copies. In fact he only printed seven, including the proof run, and kept them all himself, seemingly to ensure that they were not totally lost to posterity. A few friends saw them, but they were never intended for the general public, which was probably a wise decision. He had been working on them between 1766 and 1772 and when in that year he sent three of them to Mme Deffand, even she, one of his keenest admirers, dismissed them, telling him he must have been delirious when he wrote them and bluntly suggesting he kept to writing letters. Then in 1779 when a rumour about their existence reached William Cole, he did admit, 'I have some strange things in my drawer even wilder than the *Castle of Otranto*, and called *Hieroglyphic Tales* – but they were not written lately.' Adding in self-defence ' ... nor, whatever they may seem, was I out of my senses.'

And 'strange things' they are. They could claim to be earliest pieces of surrealism in the English language. The eighteenth century was not ready for them; indeed they have all the hallmarks of the Monty Python team. For example, the Preface explains that, 'The Hieroglyphic Tales were undoubtedly written before the creation of the world, and have ever since been preserved, by oral tradition, in the mountains of Grampcraggiri, an uninhabited island, not yet discovered.' Even Swift would have been hard pressed to surpass that. But putting Swift and Walpole alongside each other makes us immediately aware of one important difference: Swift was a satirist; Horace was not.

In satire there is always a moral, political or religious underlying ideal against which the follies or deviations of the narrative are to be measured and shown to fall short. Horace's *Hieroglyphic Tales* have no such sub-text. They were written for amusement only. In a brief Postscript he calls them 'whimsical trifles' which 'deserve at most to be considered as an attempt to vary the stale and beaten class of stories and novels, which, though works of invention, are almost always devoid of imagination.' In this we are reminded of his Preface to *Otranto* where he lamented that in prose fiction 'the great resources of fancy have been dammed up by strict adherence to common life.'

And this at a time when Fielding, Richardson and Sterne were shaping the future of the English novel, but it was not a genre which held much interest for Horace. His library contained thousands of plays and poems, but very little fiction. Sterne he found 'insipid and tedious' and Richardson 'deploringly tedious.'

There is a wealth of literary, historical and fashionably social allusion in these stories, but they are not meant to *amount* to anything, or be seen as part of a coherent argument or attitude. There is no trace whatsoever of Augustan didacticism. There may be the shadow of Catherine the Great behind the murderous monarch of the opening story 'A New Arabian Nights', but it is no more than that. Horace's oriental tale is simply a comic version of Scheherazade, in which his story-telling princess, instead of fascinating and enthralling the emperor, bores him to death – quite literally. Her tale is so full of irrelevancies, digressions, tedious genealogies and non-sequiturs that he becomes bored by it all and falls asleep. At which moment she, aided by a friendly eunuch, suffocates him with pillows. She then becomes empress and decides to continue the bedtime tradition of having a new lover every night, but 'was graciously pleased also, upon their good behaviour, to remit the subsequent execution.' And they were not even obliged to tell her stories either!

Comedy is always difficult and what is especially difficult is the sustained and seemingly-reasoned illogicality of the surreal. Horace handles it expertly in 'The King and his Three daughters', a story in which, like Lear, a king must decide which of his three daughters is to succeed him. The youngest had only one leg and bad teeth. The middle one had a strong Yorkshire accent which clearly ruled her out. The eldest, however, was 'extremely handsome, had a great deal of wit and spoke French in perfection.' Unfortunately, she had never actually been born, yet according to protocol, this eldest daughter had to be married first. Some authorities argued that as there was no eldest princess, the second must be first, but said others, if there was no first and she could not be second if she was first, 'it followed by every idea of law that she could be nobody at all.'

One day, amid all the debates surrounding this complex situation, there arrived in the Kingdom the Prince of Quifferiquimini (a name which looks as though it could be translated as 'Little Venus Mound' – but surely not!) This prince had three legs, spoke only Egyptian and, unfortunately, had been dead for some time. Naturally, the youngest princess, having only one leg, was thrilled at the appearance of one with three, but he soon set his heart on the eldest girl. The King was delighted at the prospect of such a match, but the Church objected, 'A woman that never was, and a man that had been, being deemed first cousins in the eye of canon law.' However, the situation was resolved when the second daughter ran off with a dry-salter and the citizens happily proclaimed them King and Queen, despite her Yorkshire accent.

As it is not always easy to appreciate another person's sense of humour, to relate to that of another age can at times be nigh impossible – viz old copies of Punch. And it is hard to find anything amusing about 'The Peach in Brandy', a story in which a Queen miscarries with twins and ends with a Catholic archbishop swallowing down a pickled foetus mistaking it for a peach in brandy, and the embryo's sister calling out, 'Mama, the gentleman has eat my little brother!' Having written such a story is weird enough, but weirder still is that Horace sent it to Lord Ossory in 1771 describing it simply as 'this foolery', when Lady

Ossory herself had just miscarried of twins. The Tale has as its sub-title 'This tale was written for Anne Liddel, Countess of Ossory, wife of John Fitzpatrick, Earl of Ossory. They had a daughter ANNE, the subject of his story.' Anne was aged three at the time. It is not known what the family's reaction was, but Horace had written a compassionate letter to Lady Ossory that same day and again ten days later beginning, 'I am a little impatient, Madam, to hear of your perfect recovery' and ending 'Adieu! my Lord and Lady tell me you are both well – I will not plague you again.' Which suggests they had, understandably, remained silent on the matter.

Happily, this is the only story of such a nature, yet there are others with characters whose names are quite as suggestive as Quifferiquimini – the heroine of 'The Dice Box' is called Pissimissi, which we are told signifies 'The Waters of Jordan', but in the eighteenth century a Jordan was a chamber pot, so the name is not as charming as this would suggest.

Pissimissi's adventures cry out for some Disney animation. She travels to the Court of King Solomon in a pistachio-shell chariot drawn by an elephant and a ladybird, gathering to herself as she goes a wonderful assortment of things: ninety-two dolls, seventeen baby-houses, six cart-loads of sugar-plums, a thousand ells of gingerbread, eight dancing dogs, a bear and a monkey. But as they near their goal, disaster strikes when their whole entourage is promptly swallowed up and then as promptly disgorged by a hummingbird, an event which inspires Solomon to begin his Song of Solomon: 'What he had seen – I mean all that had come out of the hummingbird's throat had made such a jumble in his ideas that there was nothing to which he did not compare all Pissimissi's beauties.' A shade blasphemous perhaps, but only a shade, and one cast by the joyous irrationality of it all.

In 'Mi Li, a Chinese Fairy Tale', the hero, Mi Li (My lie?) a Chinese Prince, is told of a series of seemingly impossible things he must discover in order to meet the love of his life. They include a bridge with no water under it, a tomb with no body in it, and a subterraneous passage in which there were dogs with eyes of rubies and emeralds. After many false trails, he chances, purely by accident, on Park-Place, the estate of Horace's cousin, Henry Conway, 'the most courteous person alive', where he finds that such things are indeed features of Conway's fashionably landscaped garden. Horace even explains the whole puzzle in a series of Notes: that the bridge was built to carry the Henley road and so allow easy access to the grounds on either side; that there was a 'fictitious tomb in a beautiful spot by the river'; and oddest of all that 'there is such a passage [in fact it was 275 yards long] cut through a chalk hill and when dogs are in the middle, the light from the mouth makes their eyes appear in the manner here described.' The whole point of the story, we realise, has been leading up to this elegant tribute to Conway and to his niece, Caroline Campbell, who proves to be the 'princess' whom Mi Li had all along been seeking, 'borne on the wings of love.'

It has been suggested by the American scholar Martin Kallich that these tales, 'could be explored seriously for evidence of the nature and content of the author's mind and imagination.' But such analysis would probably discover exactly whatever it had set out to discover. Rather than explore them, it might be better simply to enjoy them and thus discover that as well as writing history, art criticism, horror novels and melodrama, Horace

Walpole could equally be serious or whimsical, sometimes quite indecent and sometimes delightfully nonsensical in ways which would seem to be deliberately running counter to most of what is contained and implied in the term Augustan.

Running counter could be said to be characteristic of Horace and is behind his coining of a word which itself seems such a part of him. It makes its first appearance in a letter to Mann of January 1754: 'I once read a silly fairy tale, called *The Three Princes of Serendip*: as their highnesses travelled, they were always making discoveries, by accident and sagacity, of things that they were not in quest of: for instance, one of them discovered that a mule blind of the right eye had travelled the same road lately, because the grass was eaten only on the left side, where it was worse than on the right – now do you understand *serendipity*?' He also defines it as '*accidental sagacity*' (for you must observe that *no* discovery of a thing you *are* looking for, comes under this description.' How could we manage without such a word?

11

THE THOMAS CHATTERTON AFFAIR

THE NAME HENRY WALLIS PROBABLY MEANS very little to most people today, but he painted one of the most popular and instantly recognisable pictures in the Tate Gallery: *The Death of Chatterton*. Ruskin in his *Academy Notes* described it as 'faultless and wonderful'. It is certainly unforgettable: that pale and beautiful boy, lying on his narrow bed, languorously elegant in death; those plum-coloured trousers, the vial of poison and all those shreds of torn-up paper on the floor. It is tragic and, in the true sense of the word, pathetic, and the story it tells is archetypal.

The picture was painted in 1856, by which time Thomas Chatterton was not only long-dead, but also long-established as a legend, a case-history in the poetic book of martyrs. Wordsworth in 'Resolution and Independence' had famously called him 'Chatterton, the marvellous boy'. Keats had dedicated 'Endymion' to his memory and written a sonnet to him, that 'Dear child of sorrow – son of Misery', and Shelley, in 'Adonais', his memorial to Keats, had referred to him as one of the 'inheritors of unfulfill'd renown'.

Why all these elegies? Why all this fuss – and few things are more fussily extravagant than Coleridge's early 'Monody on the Death of Chatterton' – it is difficult to say. Chatterton's poems, pleasing though they are, would scarcely seem to justify it, but he had, when Wallis painted his picture, become a legend, indeed a myth, and there is no rationalising with things of that nature. The closing years of the eighteenth century were seeing some major changes taking place: a new emphasis on the individual, on the power and use of the imagination as opposed to reason. There were new and differing political ideals, a greater social awareness and benevolence, and new money was bringing about changes in the hitherto rigid class system. Chatterton was being held up as a symbol of much of that: a young and underprivileged poet of courage and imagination, who had tragically been destroyed by the conservative materialism of the time, the materialism which Blake railed so strongly against. He was hailed in retrospect as the First Romantic, and as the Herald of the Gothic Revival. But if he had been destroyed – driven to suicide – then someone (and this is an attitude we recognise all too clearly today) then someone must be to blame; must, what's more, be held *responsible*. And the blame, at that time, fell squarely and unfairly on Horace Walpole.

***

Thomas Chatterton was born in Bristol in 1752, some three or four months after the death of his unsuccessful schoolmaster father. His widowed mother, who is said to have been mentally unstable, earned what she could by taking in sewing. It was not an auspicious start to life and it got no better. From what we are told of his childhood it seems that he might have been somewhat autistic, but mooning around in the Church of St Mary Redcliff, where his uncle was sexton, he discovered a chest of old documents. The discovery was to determine the rest of his short life. They fascinated him, especially the old lettering. The timing of such a discovery was just right. Old things were, paradoxically, the new thing – especially old ruins. The tumble-down ruins of an ancient priory seen at twilight were so much more beautiful and sublime than the rigid lines of classical architecture. And if there were not enough ruins to go round, then you could always build 'em. And built they were. So, if fake ruins could be built, why couldn't fake poems be written? Hadn't Macpherson almost got away with *Ossian*?

Chatterton began, it would seem, to imagine that he lived in the age in which these things had been written and gradually even assumed the personality of a medieval monk, giving himself the name of Thomas Rowley. Before long he was writing poems by this same Rowley, couched in a pseudo olde-worldly script on sheets of ancient parchment. To his delight he even managed to fool a local bibliophile into buying them. Always full of his own self-importance, and feeling that he was entitled to recognition and respect, he had now outwitted one figure of authority, so why not aim higher? Parcelling some of these poems up together with a lengthy discourse entitled 'The Ryse of Peyncteynge yn Englâde, wroten by T. Rowlie' he had them delivered to Horace Walpole.

That Walpole should have fallen for this ruse is not altogether surprising. How could he have suspected that a letter beginning, 'Sir, Being versed a little in Antiquitys, I have met with several

Curious manuscripts ... ' had been written by a penniless sixteen year old living in the provinces? But this was a very remarkable sixteen year old. He had done his research and chosen his 'victim' very carefully, tantalisingly suggesting in his letter that the Discourse might be of use to him in any future edition of his 'Anecdotes of Painting'. That was exactly what Walpole needed. Also the Discourse seemed to contain certain proof of his theory that oil paints had been invented in England. There was also the added bait that several of the 'old' poems would have looked so very tempting to the founder of the Strawberry Press. His reply was perhaps over-hasty, but he assumed that he was corresponding with a scholar and his tone is courtesy itself: 'I have not the happiness of understanding the Saxon language and without your learned notes should not have been able to comprehend Rowley's text.' But he should at least have noticed the misuse of capital letters and the absurdity of spellings such as *Peyncteynge*. He went on to ask to see more of Rowley's poems, adding that he 'should not be sorry to print them.'

It is easy to imagine Chatterton's delight; this was more than he could ever have hoped for. He had been addressed as an equal and his fantasies had been accepted as genuine. But in his delight, he blundered and over-played his hand. He sent more poems, but revealed his identity and went so far as to ask Walpole if he could use his influence to gain him some better and more remunerative employment. He was, in effect, asking Walpole to be his patron. His suspicions raised, Walpole showed the poems to Thomas Gray, who was something of an expert in such things and he had no hesitation in declaring them to be forgeries bordering on gibberish. As he pointed out, the grammar was totally faulty, 'so haveth I', the rhymes (go/trow) would not have been valid in the 15th century, and most damning of all, this medieval monk seemed surprisingly well-read in Spenser, Shakespeare, Pope, and even Gray himself!

Walpole at first suspected that Chatterton had been put up to this and that there were those behind it who wanted him caught out and ridiculed. Ridicule was, as we have seen, something he always feared. It was a view shared by his friend Michael Lort, '... he could not help concluding that the whole thing was a fiction, contrived by one or more literary wags, who wished to impose on his credulity and to laugh at him if they succeeded and that Chatterton was only the instrument employed.' This being so, what is surprising is that Horace replied at all and so generously.

The reply has not survived but he recalled it in a later account of the whole affair: 'I wrote him a letter with as much kindness and tenderness as if I had been his guardian...and urged him, that in duty and gratitude to his mother, who had straightened herself to breed him up to a profession, he ought to labour in it, that in her old age he might absolve his filial debt. I told him also ... better judges were by no means satisfied with the authenticity of his MSS.'

He would undoubtedly have been angry and the tone of his letter may well have been more patronising than he claimed. His advice reminds us of Lockhart's contemptuous review of Keats in the *Edinburgh Magazine* in which he called him a cockney and told him to 'go back to the Shop Mr John, back to the plasters, pills and ointment boxes.'

Chatterton was incensed, feeling that Walpole's change in attitude was due entirely to snobbery and he set his mind on revenge. Only his sister's intervention prevented him from sending Walpole a poem beginning:

> Walpole! I thought not I should ever see
> So mean a heart as thine has proved to be;
> Thou who in luxury nurs'd behold'st with scorn
> The boy who friendless, penniless, forlorn
> Asks thy high favour – thou mayst call me cheat –
> Say, disdst thou ne'er indulge in such deceit?
> Who wrote Otranto?

And Chatterton, one must admit, has a fair point here. Walpole's title page read: *The Castle of Otranto, a Story translated by William Marshall from the Original Italian of Onuphrio Muralto Canon of St Nicholas at Otranto.* And the Preface to the first edition began, 'The following work was found in the library of an ancient catholic family in the north of England.' It was only in the second edition that he confessed to the subterfuge, explaining that his diffidence was due to 'the novelty of the event!' He knew that nothing of this kind had been attempted before and if it had flopped, he would have been exposed, he feared, to ridicule. Even when it was an established genre, 'forgery' of this kind was to become almost a convention of Romantic novels.

It does need to be positively pointed out that Chatterton was not the ill-used, marvellous boy celebrated by those who never knew him. He may have been a prodigy, but he was, according to his biographer, E.H.W. Meyerstein, an 'acrimonious prodigy', who behaved 'throughout his short life, to almost everyone with whom he came into contact with spitefulness and dishonesty.'

Acrimony there certainly was in Chatterton's reply: 'I think myself injured, Sir, and did you not know my circumstances you would not dare to treat me thus.' *Dare*! Walpole would not have tolerated such impertinence, but he chose this time to ignore it and returned the MSS, as asked, without further comment, probably thinking that was the end of the affair. Chatterton also felt slighted in that it had taken him so long to return his papers, but Walpole had been away in France for six weeks and had dealt with the matter immediately on his return.

But Chatterton was still not prepared to let it drop. In April 1770 he arrived in London and began writing satires and lampoons for the *Town and Country Magazine*, a rather scurrilous journal which ran features exposing liaisons and affairs of the famous and holding people up to ridicule. Chatterton wrote several attacks on *Baron Otranto*, some in verse. The lines his sister had prevented him from sending had continued

> But I will not chide
> Scorn will I repay with Scorn and Pride with Pride,
> Still, Walpole, still thy Prosy Chapters write,
> And twaddling Letters to some Fair indite,
> Laud all above thee – Fawn and Cringe to those
> Who, for thy Fame, were better Friends than Foes.
> Had I the Gifts of Wealth and Lux'ry shar'd
> Not poor and Mean – Walpole! thou hadst not dared
> Thus to insult, but I shall live and stand
> By Rowley's side – when Thou art dead and Damned.

It is interesting that Walpole's reputation as a letter-writer seems to have been known even in Bristol and by a teenager.

Whether Walpole was aware of Chatterton's attacks on him we do not know, but he was not, we do know, aware of

Chatterton's suicide, only learning of it from a chance remark by Goldsmith some nine months later.

It is a tragic story: a young man of obvious talent driven to his death by failure, debts, despair and gonorrhoea. It also has to be born in mind that according to Meyerstein, his biographer, his mental condition was so unstable that he might have killed himself at any time and there is no evidence that he was starving and he evidently had enough money to buy poison.

The death of an impoverished teenager would hardly have been of note, but it was soon to become so. As has often been observed, an early tragic death can prove to be a brilliant career move – *viz:* Jimi Hendrix and Sylvia Plath. Myths are sure to follow and to be believed. The Rowley poems began to be handed about and as was the case with *Ossian,* argument and controversy as to their authenticity soon followed, attracting ever-increasing attention. An edition of the poems appeared in 1777 and then an article in the *Monthly Review* which brought Walpole into the debate.

> Chatterton went to London and carried all his treasure with him, in hopes, we may very reasonably suppose, of disposing of it to his advantage; he accordingly applied, as I have been informed, to that learned antiquary, Mr Horace Walpole, but met with little or no encouragement from him; soon after which, in a fit of despair, as it is supposed, put an end to his unhappy life.

This is clearly wrong on two points. Chatterton never personally approached Walpole and far from it being *soon*, it was two years later that Chatterton killed himself. Nevertheless, one can see that it had the makings of a promising story: a heartless aristocrat treats an impoverished genius with contempt and so drives him to his death. In a later edition of 'Miscellanies in Prose and Verse of Thomas Chatterton' there was a clear attack on the 'gentleman well known in the republic of letters'. Readers were invited to 'feel some indignation against the person by whom he (Chatterton) was treated with neglect and contempt.' The story took hold, gaining such momentum that in 1787 Anne Seward, the poetical *Swan of Lichfield*, is calling Walpole 'that fastidious and unfeeling being, to whose insensibility we owe the extinction of the greatest poetic luminary, if one may judge by the brightness of its dawn, that ever rose in our or perhaps any other literature.' The hyperbole is enough to make one gasp and stretch one's eyes. But by 1806 she had had the opportunity of reading Horace's letters and so, coming to a fuller understanding of him, in a letter to a Miss Fenn she declares, 'His epistles have taught me to love and delight in the man whom I so long detested for his apparently unfeeling conduct towards the ill-starred Chatterton.' Now she realised that he was 'in no way answerable for that disastrous event.'

But for Walpole the early criticisms had been hurtful. As he wrote in a letter of July 1778 to William Mason, 'You know how gently I treated him. He was a consummate villain and had gone enormous lengths before he destroyed himself. It would be cruel indeed if one were to be deemed the assassin of every rogue that miscarries in attempting to cheat one.' In four long essays in the *Gentleman's Magazine*, he gave a detailed account of the actual events. He is generous in his estimation of Chatterton's talents, but the destruction of the case against him is masterly. No barrister could have presented it more cogently. But truth can be tedious and one cannot help feeling, however, that at times he doth protest overmuch. It is rather unfair to suggest that had Chatterton lived he might have gone on to commit acts of criminal forgery. Understandably, people preferred the myth and so it continued for the rest of his life, and beyond it, to be the albatross which hung about his neck.

If only Chatterton had called the poems 'imitations', it could all have been so different. Horace might well have been delighted with them, might have published them on the Strawberry Hill press and established the young man's reputation on a more solid footing.

12

THE LETTER-WRITER

IT IS OFTEN SAID – PERHAPS TOO often – that the eighteenth century was the golden age of letter-writing, but a distinction needs to be made between letter-writing and correspondence. When the Roman poet Horace wrote his letters he no more expected a reply than did St Paul, but when Horace Walpole sat down to write a letter, it would frequently be in reply to one he had received and he would be expecting a reply in return. Correspondence is a two-way thing and indeed some of his exchanges with friends amounted to hundreds of letters. But correspondence cannot take place without a postal system and it was the introduction of that which enabled and prompted the eighteenth century to become such a golden age.

The General Post Office had been founded in 1660 by Charles II in the first year of his reign, but it was not until the early years of the eighteenth century that mail coaches began to operate. Initially they ran only between London and Bath, but it was not long before they were to be seen in almost every town in the country. The arrival of the post-boy in Olney is vividly recounted by William Cowper in the opening lines of Book IV of his poem

'The Task', published in 1785.

> Hark! 'tis the twanging horn! o'er yonder bridge
> That with its wearisome but needful length
> Bestrides the wintry flood, in which the moon
> Sees her unwrinkled face reflected bright,
> He comes, the herald of a noisy world,
> With spattered boots, strapp'd waist, and frozen locks,
> News from all nations lumb'ring at his back.
> True to his charge the close-pack'd load behind,
> Yet careless what he brings, his one concern
> Is to conduct it to the destin'd inn,
> And having dropp'd th'expected bag – pass on.

The speed with which post went from one end of the country to the other is surprising. Henry Conway sent Horace a poem from Sterling in Scotland on 18 October 1746 and Horace had received it, read it and referred to it in a reply dated from Windsor on 24th. Even more surprising is the speed with which letters crossed the continent. On 21 August in that same year a letter from Mann in Florence refers to a letter Horace had written on the 7th and post from London would be in Paris after only four days.

The excitement we sense in Cowper's lines – and he was not a man by temperament much given to excitement – shows how important letters were to him. And he was not alone in this. Frequently in collections we come upon letters deeply concerned with just how letters were to be written. There was an etiquette. As Pope had put it in his 'Essay on Criticism':

> True Ease in Writing comes from Art not Chance,
> And those move easiest who have learned to dance.

Robert Dodsley in 1755 asserted, 'Letter writing rejects all pomp of words and is most agreeable when most familiar' and Cowper, writing to his cousin, Lady Hesketh, said, 'When I read your letters, I hear you talk and I love talking letters dearly.' Horace added his voice, telling Lord Lincoln, 'I have no patience with people who do not write just as they talk.' We hear these words echo down the ages and by Jane Austen's day it had become a truism she could satirise: 'I have now attained the true art of letter-writing, which we are always told, is to express on paper exactly what one would say to the same person by word of mouth.' And of course the epistolary novel had become such a feature that Fielding could satirise it in 1741 with his *Shamela*.

In Cowper's letters there is a recurrent – it would be misleading to call it *familiar* – tone of voice as he had a very limited circle of acquaintance and they all shared his rather sombre religious outlook, but Horace had an extraordinary range of friends, colleagues and associates and varied his tone to suit their different personalities and interests.

Lytton Strachey – usually so astute – was clever but wrong when he wrote of his letters, 'His writing, as he might have said himself, is like lace, the material is of very little consequence; the embroidery is all that matters.' Embroidery there certainly is, but the end-product often approaches closer to a tapestry. We do not read Strachey's letters, nor those of Virginia Woolf, for news of the Battle of Britain or for details of the wartime butter ration, but historians go to Horace's letters to Mann in order to learn exactly what had happened in parliament, how politicians had voted, how they reacted to each other and what was being said of battles – the Jacobite uprising for example. To Horace and Mann, these events were *news*, and now as we turn the pages, so the eighteenth century rolls before our eyes, eminent and brilliant persons and momentous events.

Writing to the antiquary John Fenn he made his views very clear, 'Familiar letters written by eye-witnesses, and that, without design, disclose circumstances that let us more immediately into important events, are genuine history, and as far as they go, more satisfactory than formal premeditated narratives.'

Horace knew that he was not, by reason of health and personality, able to take an active role in life, but he could record it for posterity. As he declared to Conway as early as June 1760, 'I have everything in the world to tell posterity.' And albeit something of an exaggeration, Strachey was on the right lines when he suggested that, 'His correspondence was his serious occupation; he didn't snatch moments from life to write letters, he snatched moments from letter writing in which to live.' To be a really great letter-writer, he added, ' it is not enough to write an occasional excellent letter; it is necessary to write constantly, indefatigably with ever-recurring zeal.' These conditions Horace certainly met. Writing to Mann in August 1784 he announced, 'I have been counting how many letters I have written to you since I landed in England in 1741 – they amount – astonishingly! to above 800 and we have not met in three and forty years! A correspondence of near half a century is, I suppose, not to be paralleled in the history of the Post Office.' And Mann's contribution is close to a thousand. Very early in their correspondence Horace had asked Mann to return his letters to him. We only know this, however, from Mann's reply in which he says he would be 'vastly glad' to do so and encouraging him to go on with the great work he had in hand. In the published version of Horace's letter there is no mention of such a request. He did not, we can assume, want his readers to know that he had edited and sometimes re-written them. From this we can judge that his letters were always intended equally for that 'undutiful wretch posterity'. His scheme was no secret from his friends, it would seem, as Gray – cynical as ever – gave it his lukewarm encouragement: 'you need not fear but posterity will be ever glad to know the absurdity of their ancestors.'

That first meeting between Mann and Horace in 1739 proved to be of greater importance than either can have foreseen. As the holder of a diplomatic post, Mann would have needed to be kept informed of the political situation in England and who better to do so than Horace, who was not only the son of the Prime Minister, but someone who, for his own reasons, wished to record them. It was a perfect match. The choice of correspondents was a conscious decision on Horace's part as we can tell from a letter he sent to George Montagu in 1764, apologising for not having written and explaining that he had no news except politics and 'such trash I am forced to send to Lord Hertford and Sir Horace Mann because they are out of England', adding, 'unless I can divert *you* I had rather wait until we can laugh together.' Certainly the more amusing of his letters are those to Montagu.

The eighteenth century – like every other century – had its political upheavals and traumatic events and Horace's letters to Mann record and recount them: the Jacobite Uprising, the execution of the rebel lords, the Seven Year War, the Gordon Riots, the corruption in India and the slave trade. But these letters are not the political monotone they have sometimes been declared.

There were other interests that the friends shared – art and artists, books, antiquities and collections of them. It needs to be stressed that though they never met in all those years they remained close friends and there is plenty of friendly chit-chat among the politics. When Horace was about to visit his father at Houghton he told Mann:

> Indeed I don't lay in a store of cakes and bandboxes, and citron water and cards and cold meat as country gentlewomen do after the session. My packing up and travelling concerns lie in a very small compass: nothing beyond myself and Patapan, my footman, a cloak bag and a couple of books.

Only friends write to each other like this and then there are the letters about health – usually gout.

> I have a constant pain in my breast or stomach.
> It comes like a fever at six in the morning,
> proceeds to a pain by the time that I rise ...

There is even an account of the removal of his piles.

The political accounts often have a distinctly personal element. The account of the execution of the Scottish lords, as we have seen, includes detail and dialogue enough to make us believe he was there and in the letters recounting the Uprising we learn that things were so serious that he was thinking of leaving the country.

Mann's own letters have more than once been dismissed as dull, but they too have their moments. The sudden death in 1774 of Pope Clement XIV was put down to poison and Mann spared no detail of the autopsy.

> As soon as they touched his head, all the hair and all the teeth fell

out, all the bones of his body crumbled away and the flesh upon the least touch of the knife did not divide but came away in pieces.

The Pope's taster died too and Mann put it down to the hot chocolate they had drunk! The whole piece is gruesome, but at the same time one is tempted to laugh. There is more than a hint of anti-papist feeling about it.

It is this blend of the public and the personal which makes their exchanges worth dipping into.

The variety of tone is evident throughout the 4000 letters and can be seen by looking at how a single event is reported to different people. One instance is the trial in 1760 of Laurence, Earl Ferrers, who was arraigned before his peers in the House of Lords for the murder of his steward, found guilty, unanimously, publicly hanged at Tyburn and his body handed over to the anatomists. George Montagu would have been well aware of the details of the case and Horace's letter to him of 19 April – the day after the trial – begins with the chattiest of openings: 'Well, this big week is over.' There follows only one brief reference to the trial itself, and that Ferrers had pleaded insanity. Horace's response to that is equally light-hearted: 'It was more shocking to see his two brothers brought to prove the lunacy of their own blood.' Apart from that he treats the whole scene as though it had been a social event. 'Lady Conway was there ... she and Lord Bolingbroke seemed to have very different thoughts and were acting overall the old comedy of eyes.' He felt sure that Montagu would want to know who else was there and what they were wearing: 'The Duke of Marlborough ... looked clumsy in his robes. He has new ones, he had given away his father's to the valet de chambre.' Montagu, he knows, will be familiar with these people and will be interested in the gossip. Even in a later letter the execution is dealt with quite casually: 'The horrid lunatic was dead in four minutes.'

When he wrote about it to Mann, none of the lords were mentioned as he would not have known them and would not have been interested. What Mann received prompted a thank you and the brief observation that 'The whole process, and particularly the catastrophe, is an interesting historical narrative.' And that is what it is – and it takes up a full 8 pages in the printed edition – prefaced by the assurance that, 'I am now going to give you a minute account of him.' It starts with a complete history of the Ferrers family, his wife, the failure of the marriage, his mistresses, and his children. The detail is so minute that we learn of him playing piquet for money with his warders in The Tower; that he went from The Tower to Tyburn in his 'wedding clothes'. We are given, seemingly verbatim, his conversation with the chaplain who asked his leave at least to repeat the Lord's Prayer and received the reply, 'I always thought it a good prayer, you may use it if you please.' And we are finally told that the executioners fought over the rope. Why he had written at such length he explains, 'The man, the manners of the country, the justice of so great and curious a nation, all seem to me striking, and must, I believe, do more so to you who have been absent long enough to read of your own country as history.' One cannot help feeling that it is not only Mann he is addressing here but us too and he has certainly held our attention.

Similarly when he wrote of the Coronation of George III he calls it a puppet-show in his letters to both Mann and Montagu, but whereas he regales Montagu with acerbic barbs about most of the puppets – 'My Lady Harrington, covered with all the diamonds she could borrow ... ' – he tells Mann, 'he would say nothing of who looked well, you know them no more than if I told you of the next coronation.' One snippet of hilarity he could not resist though, ' ... behind the altar the Queen had a retiring chamber – she had occasion to go thither – in the privetest spot where she certainly did not want company, she found the Duke of Newcastle.' In Thomas Gray's version of the story we learn that he was 'perked up in the very act upon the anointed velvet close-stool.' There is more of the like when Horace writes to his close friend John Chute about the niceties of Court behaviour in France. The Queen, we are told, 'is attended by two or three old ladies, who are languishing to be in Abraham's bosom; the only man's bosom to whom they can hope for admittance.' And worse is to follow. The Dauphiness is attended by 'four Mesdames, who are clumsy, plump old wretches ... wriggling as if they wanted to make water.' The pages sparkle time and again with the unexpected and the astonishing as when he tells Bentley of a woman who was convinced that her dead daughter had 'transmigrated into a robin-redbreast.'

It is the variety of tone and topic which makes reading a collection of his letters such a pleasure. Writing to Gray from Paris in 1766 he gives a close account of various female members of the French aristocracy, including his first impressions of Mme du Deffand. It is a very level-headed account with occasional asides on the French character, such as, '... as their high opinion of their own country remains, for which they can no longer assign any reason, they are contemptuous and reserved, instead of being ridiculously, consequently pardonably, impertinent.' And this is followed closely by a letter to Montagu which begins, 'Mr Chute tells me that you have taken a new house in squireland and have given yourself up for two years more to port and parsons ... I don't care which. You will get the gout, turn Methodist and expect to ride to heaven upon your own great toe.'

Letters like this are of course fun and memorable, but Horace had many serious interests. As an antiquarian he was far from being an amateur or dilettante as we see from his correspondence with William Cole.

Although three years older than Horace and not a member of the Quadruple Alliance, Cole was a close enough friend at Eton to be invited to Horace's home in Chelsea where, as he was later to observe, Sir Robert struck him as 'a very corpulent, lusty man'. They remained friends at Cambridge, but then lost contact until 1762 when Horace's *Anecdotes of Painting in England* was published and Cole wrote to him to thank him 'for the extreme pleasure and excitement' it had given him, but adding that he had met with two or three errata and had two or three trifling observations of another kind to offer. What followed was enough to fill eleven pages in the printed edition and demonstrate not only his close reading but also the extent of his knowledge. He points out that Saffron Walden is in Sussex and not Suffolk as Horace had put it and that it was the Dean of Lincoln's 'grandmother (not his mother) who had lived to see 367 (not 365) descended from her.' Now for an author to have so many mistakes pointed out to him (and I speak from experience) is not an altogether pleasant experience, but Horace, to his great credit, not only took it on the chin, but thanked him for 'the most kind and obliging letter in the world', calling him 'a so much deeper antiquarian' and inviting him to Strawberry Hill and even asking him for more help.

Interestingly, he was nearer the truth than he realised when he added 'We both labour, I will not say for the public, for the public troubles its head very little about our labours, but for the few of posterity that shall be curious ... ' Cole was an antiquarian who loved research for its own sake, writing histories of Cambridgeshire and Buckinghamshire which totalled 114 volumes which he never attempted to have published but were left to the British Museum.

There is very little small talk in their letters, unless we register the innumerable discussions of gout, but the frequent evidence of Cole's research is everywhere: 'At page 105 of your *Richard III* you say 'could we recover the register of the births of her children...' I have recovered such a register and send you the following extracts.' What then follows is a list of eleven detailed entries. Similarly, on Horace's part, it is almost all exchanges on antiquarian matters, but there are also moments when we are at a loss to how to react. Writing of his tour of the west Country he tells Cole, 'As I descended the hill, I found in a wretched cottage a child in an ancient oaken cradle, exactly in the same form of that lately published from the cradle of Edward II. I purchased it for five shillings ... ' The total lack of feeling makes one shudder. And five shillings, when five guineas would not have hurt him.

The value Horace put on his friendship with William Cole has been underestimated. Hundreds of letters passed between them and although they held very different political and religious views they never allowed this to come between them, 'You and I differ radically in our principles, and yet in forty years they have never cast a gloom over our friendship.' Cole was also a High Church Anglican with strong leanings to Rome, but even that was overlooked, 'I like Popery as well as you and have shown that I do. I like it as I like chivalry and romance. They all furnish one with ideas and visions which Presbyterianism does not.'

It was not an entirely epistolary friendship. Cole was a frequent visitor to Strawberry Hill and in 1765 he joined Horace in Paris where – when not incapacitated by gout – they visited churches, porcelain dealers and auction houses. 'I am head over ears at Count Caylus's auction,' he wrote to Conway, 'and have bought half of it for a song.'

They also had plans to write a history of Gothic architecture and in a letter of August 1769 Horace outlined his ideas: 'With regard to the history of Gothic Architecture ... I would give a series of plates ... beginning with the round Roman arch, and going on to show how they plastered and zigzagged it and the how the ornaments crept in till the beautiful Gothic arrived at its perfection.' He then continues at some length, which is all very tantalising as nothing came of the scheme.

There is mostly a respectful ease to their letters, with one sudden and remarkable indication of Horace's affection for Cole when he rebuked him playfully for complaining about his health. 'But, Goodman Frog, if you will live in the fens ... ' Horace once said of him when his life did seem in danger, 'you who are full of nothing but gentle and generous sentiments', and as we read his letters we see how true this is. Cole was a man of great erudition and courtesy, without a trace of vanity or personal ambition; four qualities not often met with in conjunction.

Cole and Gray had one thing in common – they were both

natural scholars with a love of independent research for its own sake even if it never led anywhere – but whereas Cole was always good-natured and affable, Gray, as Horace himself put it 'was the worst company in the world ... from a melancholy turn ... from a little too much dignity ... his writings are admirable, he himself is not agreeable.' It is a terrible indictment – and from a friend. Cole kept his feelings under control – though he did say he found Gray 'disgustingly effeminate, finical and affected' – but Gray could let rip when he needed to, as he did to Horace, we remember, when he learned that Dodsley intended including a portrait of him in the edition of his poems: 'Sir, you are not out of your wits! This I know, if you suffer my head to be published you infallibly will put me out of mine ... I do assure you, if I had received such a book with such a frontispiece without any warning, I believe it would have given me a palsy.' The plan, not surprisingly, was dropped and Gray lived on.

It has been said – apropos Charles Lamb's attitude to Coleridge – that no one you have been at school with as a child is going to be able to impress you in later life and there is certainly a relaxed tone in the correspondence between Horace and Gray. There is certainly far less *performance* on Horace's part: 'It would be affected, even to you, to say that I am indifferent to fame. I certainly am not, but am quite indifferent to almost everything I have done to acquire it.'

It is a great loss that so few of Horace's letters to Gray have survived and apart from some rather desultory remarks about *Otranto* there is little of literary interest in Gray's; indeed there is, yet again, page after page about gout. Gray's most interesting letters are those he wrote to Thomas Wharton who was appointed poet laureate in 1785, a post Gray had declined in 1758 and it is perhaps not without note that it was to Wharton he sent the detailed journal he kept of his tour of the Lake District.

After Gray's death Horace's letters on literary matters were directed towards William Mason whose ability as a poet he wildly overestimated. For the most part they are not of any great interest, but are invaluable when Mason asks for his help in the *Life and Letters* (he bowdlerised the letters) *of Thomas Gray* he was planning. Horace's reply, as we have seen, dwelt at length on their falling out at Reggio and he had the humility to say that 'I treated him insolently; he loved me and I did not think he did.'

It has been suggested that as one recipient of a particular type of letter fell away, so Horace quickly looked for a replacement and this may partly explain the letters to Mason. It might also explain those to Lady Ossory. When his exchange with Montagu dried up he needed someone to send snippets of social news to and she was at that time perfect for the part.

Although there are letters to her as early as 1765, the real correspondence began in 1771 when she was thirty-five, twenty years younger than Horace. Her life had been an eventful but not a happy one. At eighteen she had been married off to Augustus Henry, third Duke of Grafton, who was already credited with sixteen illegitimate children and continued to be seen openly in public with his mistress. In 1765 they separated, seemingly amicably, but then Horace introduced her, quite innocently, to the handsome young Lord Ossory who was eight years her junior. They soon became lovers and once her husband learned that she was pregnant he sued for divorce by act of parliament. It was, it seems, permissible for a man – and he was by then Prime Minister – to father sixteen illegitimate offspring, but totally unacceptable for a woman to give birth to one. She was now a social outcast and she and her young husband retired – contentedly though – to his country estate at Ampthill in Bedfordshire. She must, however, have missed the social life of London, but from then on Horace kept her informed as to all that was going on in four hundred of the most brilliant letters he ever wrote. Unfortunately, not a single one of her replies has survived, which is all the more frustrating when we read of him thanking her for her 'entertaining letter'.

There are delightful moments, as when he had been complaining about the weather and added, 'I have discovered that Nature as a compensation has given us verdure and coal-mines in lieu of summer, and as I can afford to keep a good fire and have a beautiful view from my window, why should I complain?' And writing of Margaret his housekeeper, 'She loves all creatures so well she would have been happy in the Ark and sorry when the Deluge ended.' Some acerbic moments there are, 'Miss Prim whose lips were stuffed into her nostrils.' Some bitter ones too, 'I am at last not sorry you have no son, and your daughters I hope, will be married to Americans, and not in this dirty despicable island!'

He was, as he called himself, her 'gazetteer' of social events, but he also wrote to her length about such important issues as the French Revolution, Herschel's discovery of Uranus, the Gordon Riots, the disastrous state into which Houghton had fallen and, interestingly, the attacks made on him about his dealings with Chatterton. And not once in these matters does he ever *write down* to her. One of the few things we can say for absolute certainty about Horace is that he always took women seriously.

While it can be argued that Lady Ossory replaced George Montagu, and Mason replaced Gray, the Marquise du Deffand replaced no one. She was totally herself without even a passing resemblance to anyone else on the planet. It was in October 1765 when he was visiting Paris with William Cole that Horace first encountered Mme du Deffand at her salon in the Convent de Saint Joseph. In her youth she had been a vivacious member of the brilliant and scandalous Court at Sceaux and had briefly been the mistress of the Regent, the Duc d'Orléans. She was now sixty-eight, twenty years older than Horace, and had been totally blind for the past twelve years. His first mention of her to Conway is as 'a blind old debauchée of wit', but a friendship began. They went to Midnight Mass together on Christmas Eve and his diary shows that before long they were meeting almost every day and he refers to her as having 'all vivacity, wit, memory, judgement, passion and agreeableness' and as 'certainly the most generous friendly being upon the earth.'

By the time he left Paris in the following spring, Mme du Deffand had – there seem no other way of putting it – fallen in love with him. When he reached Chantilly he must have written to her. We do not have that letter, but we have her reply and from it we can deduce that he had been alarmed by the way she was expressing her feelings for him. He fears the ridicule he would incur if her letters were opened and read by officials, as it is now known that some of them were. She tried to put him at ease, 'I begin by assuring you of my prudence ... no one will know of our correspondence ... I will do exactly what you stipulate. I have already begun by disguising my sorrow.' But even in that letter she says, 'It is impossible to love more tenderly than I do you.'

Her feelings are understandable when we compare the days of her youth with being old and infirm, suffering from insomnia and ennui. Here was a man of wit and intelligence who made her feel alive again: 'I thought you different from anything I had ever seen; you answered to the conception I had formed of what an honourable man should be.' (d'un parfaitment honnête homme.) And yet there is something disturbing about the way she reacts. There is a curious element of role-play about it, as she seems to be claiming to be a young girl again. She refers to Horace as 'her tutor' as though their ages were reversed, and to her young carer and companion as her grandmother. One also has to wonder whether Horace had found a mother figure he could love. Aspects of *The Mysterious Mother* do come to mind.

But not to take this too far, we need to remember that he always had included several older ladies among his friends. One of the attractions of Twickenham, he had said, was that there were 'dowagers as plenty as flounders all about.' He valued their conversation and that they could regale him with stories of the past, and the past, as we have seen, often seemed to him preferable to the present. And Mme du Deffand's past, the *ancien regime*, had been exceptional and such as would never be seen again. What's more she was one of the most brilliant women of her time and her letters would, he realised, be a splendid historical record and so part of his scheme, as Mary Berry put it, 'to transmit the eighteenth century to posterity.' And she was a good letter-writer, so might not her letters rival those of his 'adored Mme de Sévigné'?

Correspondence was Horace's life's work and that letter from Chantilly was only the first of around 1700 which passed between them during the next fifteen years. But though he never admits it, he must surely have felt somewhat disappointed as most of her letters continue to be about her feelings, how much she misses him and so on, which is somewhat surprising considering that she would have had to dictate them. Yet he kept the correspondence up, week after week and visited her five times, five arduous journeys by boat and coach, journeys in which he said he was seasick, poisoned by dirt and vermin, stifled by heat and choked by dust and starved for want of anything he could bear to touch, let alone eat.

Her last letter was written on 3 August 1780 and she knew it was the end, ' ... since I am never to see you again, there is nothing I am sorry to leave ... Amuse yourself as much as you can, my friend ... you will miss me for we all like to know that we are loved.' She left Horace all her papers and she also left him her little dog Tonton which, though it had a vicious temper, was to become a great favourite.

He had made sure that all the letters he had written to her were returned to him and after his death most were wantonly destroyed by Mr Berry his executor. The few which it was decided to keep were published by Mary Berry in 1811 as *Letters of the Marquise du Deffand to the Hon. Horace Walpole*. In a review in the *Quarterly*, Charles Grant wrote, 'Some extracts are given of Mr Walpole's replies and we confess that we are almost selfish enough to wish that they occupied a greater part of these volumes.' A wish I am sure we all share.

Nevertheless we owe Mme du Deffand an incalculable debt

for the pen portrait of him which she compiled in a letter of 1776, which, long though it is, needs to be read in full.

> No, no. I cannot do your portrait. No one knows less than I do. You appear sometimes as I wish you were, sometimes as I fear you may not be, and perhaps never as you really are. It is obvious you are very intelligent in many ways. Everyone knows this as well as I, and you should be aware of it more than anyone.
>
> It is your character that should be portrayed, and that is why I cannot be a good judge: indifference or at least impartiality is essential. Yet I can vouch for your integrity. You are principled and courteous and pride yourself on firmness of purpose, so that when you make a decision, for better or worse, nothing can make you change your mind, often to the point of obstinacy. You have a good heart and your friendship is steadfast, but neither tender nor yielding. Fear of weakness hardens you; you try not to be ruled by emotions; you cannot refuse friends in dire need, you sacrifice your interests to theirs, but you deny them the smallest favours; you are kind to everyone, and to those to whom you are are concerned, you hardly bother to exert yourself. Your disposition is very pleasing, although not too equable. Your manner is noble, easy and natural; your desire to please is without affectation. Your knowledge and experience of the world have made you scorn humanity and yet you have learned to adjust: you know that outward expressions are merely insincerities; you respond with deference and good manners so that all those who do not care in the least whether you like them or not have a good opinion of you. I do not know if you have much feeling; if you do you fight it, for you think it a weakness; you allow yourself only the loftier kind. You are thoughtful, you have absolutely no vanity although plenty of self-esteem; but your self-esteem does not blind you; it leads you to exaggerate your faults rather than to hide them. You give a good opinion of yourself only if forced to do so

when comparing yourself with others. You have discernment and tact, perfect taste and faultless manners. You could have been part of the most fashionable society in centuries past; you are so now in this, and would be in those of the future. Your character derives much from your country, but your manners are equally correct everywhere. You have one weakness which is inexcusable fear of ridicule. You sacrifice your better feelings to it and let it regulate your conduct. It makes you harken to fools who give you false impressions that your friends cannot rectify. You are easily influenced, a tendency you recognise and which you remedy by adhering too strictly to principle; your determination never to give in is occasionally excessive, and over matters that are hardly worth the effort. You are noble and generous, you do good for the pleasure of doing so, without ostentation, without hope of reward; in short your soul is beautiful and good.

Addition to the Portrait, 30 November, 1766

Only truth and simplicity please you; you distrust subtleties, you hate metaphysics; large ideas bore you, and you don't much enjoy deep reflection, you think it of little use; your philosophy teaches you that it is better to suppress your emotions than to fight them. You want to do so by diversions, you mock everything, and, new Democritus, the world is nothing for you but a stage whose actors you hiss; your bent is irony; you excel in fields that demand much wit, grace and lightness. You are naturally light-hearted, but you are too sensitive and sensibility often hinders gaiety. To remedy this you seek out-of-the-ordinary ways to occupy and amuse yourself. You build exotic houses, you raise monuments to a king of brigands, you pretend to have forbearance, etc. etc. Lastly, you seem a little mad in your eccentricities which are, however, the product of reason. I cannot say anything about your dislike of friendship; it is apparently founded on some deep sorrow, but as you are only vague about this, one is led to believe that you are afraid, or else wish to establish a rule of conduct, as little without foundation as all your rules which you do not follow despite your eloquence, because your precepts are not backed up by your practice. You have friends, you are entirely devoted to them; their interests are yours; all your talk and all your reasoning against friendship fail to convince them that you are not, of all people in the world, the most capable of it.

It is a remarkable letter and proof in itself of what an astute, perceptive and highly intelligent woman she was. Small wonder that Horace so enjoyed her company. Who would not?

Her death in 1780 was a great sadness to Horace, but more were to follow. He had already lost his close friends Chute and Gray, but within a very few years George Montagu died, to be followed by William Cole, then Kitty Clive and in 1786 by one his oldest friends and long-time correspondent Horace Mann. Life was not going smoothly. In 1791, his nephew, George, who had become quite insane, eventually died and Horace, perforce, became Lord Orford. The Houghton estate was, in his own words, 'a mortifying ruin' and he was forced to spend weeks and months dealing with lawyers and agents, coping with debts he did his best to discharge. He accepted the title but never took his seat in the Lords. To Lady Ossory he wrote, 'I am not vain of being the poorest earl in England, nor delighted to have outlived all my family.'

He was getting old. He was a bachelor with no close family. His gout was getting worse and he was lonely. Twenty years before he had written to Montagu, 'Age ought sometimes to polish itself against younger acquaintance, yet it must be the work of folly if one hopes to contract friendship with them.' There is some truth in what he says, but at the age of 73 an event occurred which showed it was not always so.

In October 1788 he wrote to Lady Ossory to tell her of a new family that had moved into the Twickenham area: a Mr Berry and his two daughters, Mary and Agnes, aged 24 and 23. Mr Berry was the son of a Scottish landowner, but he had outraged his wealthy great uncle by marrying, for love, a young woman with no fortune, and had been promptly disinherited. His wife died leaving him with the two girls to bring up, but his younger brother, to his great credit, gave him £800 a year, quite enough in those days to ensure a comfortable life. William Shenstone lived well and managed to create the splendid gardens at The Leasowes on only £300.

Mr Berry broke with convention yet again and decided to undertake his daughters' education himself, taking them to France and Italy for three years, with the result, as Horace explained, that 'They are the best informed and the most perfect creatures I ever saw at their age. They are exceedingly sensible, entirely natural and unaffected, frank and being able to talk on any subject.' The latter attribute being guaranteed to win Horace's admiration and approval. It must have been obvious to Lady Ossory, as it is to us, that he had been swept off his feet, particularly, as it transpired, by Mary. He enclosed a copy of the verses he had had printed for them when they visited Strawberry Hill.

> Still would his press their fame record,
> So amiable the pair is!
> But, oh! how vain to think *his* word
> Can add a straw to Berry's!

A delightful set of puns, but he asked her not to let anyone else see them in case it made him look ridiculous and we know how fearful he was of that happening. What saved him was that there were two of them, ' ... were there but one of you, I should be ashamed of being so strongly attached at my age; but being in love with both I glory in my passion, and think it a proof of my sense.'

They were an exceptional pair (though Mary was always the favourite) combining great personal charm with intellectual ability, and they not only admired Strawberry Hill, they adorned it. When they went away – visiting family in Yorkshire or the seaside at Lymington – he missed their company and wrote almost daily: 'It was a sweet consolation to the short time I may have left to fall into such society; no wonder then that I am unhappy at that consolation being abridged.' He was lonely without them: 'I have not spoken to a single person but my servants since we parted last night.'

When they left for an extended tour of the continent, he became increasingly anxious and with good reason considering the troubled state France was in. His letters are full of concern for their safety, but there are some delightful moments too. In 1791 'Boswell's book', as he called it was published and did not impress him: 'It is a new kind of libel by which you may abuse anybody by saying that some dead person said so and so about somebody. Often indeed Johnson made the most brutal speeches to living persons, for though he was good natured at bottom he was very ill-natured at top ... Johnson's blind Toryism and known brutality kept me aloof, nor did I ever exchange a syllable with him. Nay, I do not think I was ever in a room with him six times in my days.'

The Berry sisters had one particularly special quality and that is that they were great listeners and clearly enjoyed Horace's remembrances and anecdotes such that he wrote *Reminiscences written in 1788 for the Amusement of Miss Mary and Miss Agnes Berry*. It is not very amusing now, even in the eighteenth-century use of the word; the intricacies of political life being of interest only to professional historians, but he was confident that the Berry sisters would enjoy it, which tells us a good deal about them. As he put it himself, it was 'penned for the Amusement of a Pair of such sensible and cultivated minds as I never met at so early an age & whose pretty eyes I do know will read me with candour.' And in it he addresses them personally as though it were a letter, his favourite and most accomplished form of writing.

Among the parade of forgotten dukes and lords, and their wives and mistresses, there are moments when the gossip catches our attention: Lady Sundon was 'an absurd and pompous simpleton'. And there are stories we are delighted to be told – that George II happily believed the Queen's extensive improvements to the gardens at Richmond were being paid for out of her own money, while in fact Horace's father had been financing her out of the Treasury to the tune of some £20,000. Small wonder that he always felt he could count on her support. There are also some surprising snippets of history, such as William III's idea of bringing the Pretender, then still a child, back to England, educating him up as a Protestant and leaving the crown to him. What a difference to our history that scheme would have made.

There can be little doubt as to the happiness the Berry sisters brought to the closing years of Horace's life. But it had to close. In July 1796 he wrote to Lady Ossory, 'How many poor old wretches are there who suffer more, and who have none of my comforts and assistances, though probably deserving them more.' In November however, during a particularly cold spell of weather he became seriously ill and was taken back to London. The Berry's went with him. Sad to say, he suffered badly before eventually dying on 2nd March, Lord Glenervie recording in his diary, 'his condition was lamentable and his death a real relief to himself and his friends.'

Final proof of the high estimation in which he held Mary and Agnes is evident from his will. He not only bequeathed them Little Strawberry Hill in which they had been living for some years and £4,000, but appointed them as his literary executors, leaving all his published and unpublished papers to them. The handsome five quarto volumes of his *Works* published in 1798, largely the work of Mary, have never been superseded and were reprinted as late as 1999.

13

ARIEL THE SPRITE

AS MARK ANTONY SAID, WHEN PEOPLE die, 'the good is oft interred with their bones', and thirty years after Horace's interment Macaulay could still hardly find a good word to say about him. In what purported to be a review of his Letters to Horace Mann, in the *Edinburgh Review* of October 1832, he makes only brief and passing references to the letters themselves, devoting instead some 8000 words to attacks on him from every possible angle, but chiefly on his personality. Half way through he does concede that Horace's works 'have real merit', but quickly follows this up by asserting that 'there is scarcely any writer in whose works it would be possible to find so many contradictory judgements, so many sentences of extravagant nonsense'.

There is no question but that Macaulay's review is a brilliant piece of writing, a masterly polemic. It begins with a nasty but unforgettable image. After praising the culinary excellence of pâté-de-foie-gras, he then adds that ' ... it would be nothing if it were not made out of livers preternaturally swollen, so none but an unhealthy and disorganised mind could have produced such literary luxuries as the works of Walpole.'

As W.S. Lewis observed, Macaulay's essay has had more influence on Walpole's reputation than all other comments on him combined. Some of his generalisations are, however, so sweeping as to be absurd: 'Everybody who reads his works with attention will find that they swarm with loose and foolish observations.' Can he have read the *Reminiscences*? There are others which seem bent on simply being malicious. Quoting the motto which Horace had humorously appended to his *Catalogue of Royal and Noble Authors* 'Where the Devil, Sir Ludovico, did you collect so many imbecilities?', he suggests it should be inscribed on the title page of all his books and over every door of Strawberry Hill, which elsewhere he declares to be 'a grotesque house with pie-crust battlements.'

Some of his assertions are also blatantly untrue and unsupportable: 'About politics he knew nothing and cared nothing.' This about a man who was an MP of 27 years standing, who said in his *Memoirs of George II*, that he thought himself, 'qualified to give some account of transactions, which few men have known better and of which scarce any can speak with equal impartiality.' Likewise, Macaulay claimed, 'When he recorded gossip, he fancied he was writing history', whereas Sir Leslie Stephen's view was that, 'the history of England throughout a very large segment of the eighteenth century is simply a synonym for the works of Horace Walpole.'

There is an element of truth in some of what he said. It is certainly true that Horace's literary judgements and evaluations of contemporary writers can be bizarre. He makes not a single reference to William Cowper, although his *John Gilpin* (1782) and *The Task* (1785) had made him the most popular poet in

England. But as he had once observed to Mann, 'I cannot bear modern poetry.' And that he rated Mason and Conyers Middleton above Collins, Richardson and Fielding beggars belief. It may well be true, as Lytton Strachey suggested that, 'literature amused him, it interested him, but it never moved him.'

It is also surprising that a declared republican should have written at such length about royal authors, but it is bizarre on Macaulay's part to accuse him of being, 'frightened into a fanatical royalist' when 'the revolutionary spirit really began to stir in Europe.' The bloody September massacres in Paris were hardly likely to enhance a spirit of Republicanism, any more than the British Communist Party managed to survive the truth about Stalin's atrocities or the final downfall of the Soviet Union.

The most lasting damage to Horace's reputation was the dismissal of him as a trifler and dilettante, totally lacking in seriousness. 'Affectation is the essence of the man,' Macaulay insisted. But as Lytton Strachey put it, describing the essay with his customary wit and brilliance, ' ... the paragraphs go off like Catherine Wheels; everything is present that could be desired except the remotest understanding of the subject.' What Strachey understood was that, 'The masks he wore were imposed upon him by his caste, by his breeding, by his own innate sense of the decencies and proprieties of life.'

What Macaulay had failed to understand was exactly that, what it meant to be a gentleman in the eighteenth century. He doubtless thought that it was no more than his due when he himself was made a lord in 1857, but Horace would not have believed such a thing possible and the very notion that a poet, even the poet laureate, could be elevated to the peerage would have seemed ludicrous to him. A gentleman could not be *made*. What bothered Horace was quite the reverse: whether, as a gentlemen, he really ought to be parading himself as an author. In his day the only recognisable occupations for a gentleman were hunting, shooting, fishing, gambling and adultery and he had already made himself conspicuous by failing to participate in any of them.

Another prong of Macaulay's attack is that Horace, 'was a bundle of inconsistencies ... his features were covered by mask within mask ... he played innumerable parts and overplayed them all.' While it is true that he adopted a different attitude and tone in his letters according to whom he was writing, that is only natural. Everyone does it. They were not masks, but evidence of his many interests and abilities. His was not the age of micro-specialisms we see among today's academics. The contents of Strawberry Hill – from the bronze eagle to Cromwell's hat – show that there were few things he was not interested in. As well as being one of the most acclaimed of all letter-writers, he can also be said to be an antiquary, a novelist, a poet, a social charmer, a gardener, a political and historical chronicler, and a playwright. And that is to say nothing of Strawberry Hill itself. This was where the problem lay. As Chesterfield had warned his son, 'Wear your learning, like your watch, in a private pocket, and do not pull it out and strike it, merely to show you have one.' A gentleman should never be conspicuous, certainly not for his abilities, and least of all for his intellectual ability.

Of course, the attitude Lord Chesterfield was advocating was not new. It can be dated back to such Renaissance 'courtesy books' as Castiglioni's *The Courtier* of 1528, in which he emphasises the need for *Sprezzatura*. Originally an art term denoting the seemingly effortless brushwork of a supreme master, it later became the term for that degree of nonchalance which was taken to be the hallmark of the consummate courtier. For example, a courtier might be expected to be an accomplished musician, but:

> ... let our courtier come to show his music as a thing to pass the time withal and as he were enforced to do it ... and for all he be skilful and doth well understand it, yet will I have him to dissemble the study and pains that a man must needs take in all things that are well done. And let make semblance that he esteemeth but little in himself that quality, but in doing it exceedinglywell, make it much esteemed of other men.

There is evidence throughout Horace's letters of the study and pains which were involved in everything he undertook. He did not 'saunter through life', as was once said of him. He was always busy, agreeing with Gray that the recipe or happiness was always having something to do, 'but how few can apply it.' To Bentley he wrote, 'I am constantly occupied every minute of the day, reading, writing, forming plans ... ' His plans were no lightweight matters, being for the landscaping of his gardens and the constant changes and additions to Strawberry Hill. And as for his writing – there are the five hefty volumes of his *Works*, besides the forty of his letters.

Despite – or one might even say because of – his obvious achievement, self-deprecation would have been an automatic part of his social culture and it is there time and again in his letters. When asked for some details to go into a Biographical History of Literature, he declined, 'My life has been too insignificant to afford materials interesting to the public ... nor are my writings of a class or merit to entitle me to any distinction.' To Thomas Gray, a lifelong friend from childhood, he could afford to speak plainly, 'It would be affected, even to you, to say I am indifferent to fame, I certainly am not, but I am indifferent to almost anything I have done to deserve it.' He was in no doubt as to the extent of his achievement, but knew it was not of the highest. In his later years he declared, 'Who does not look back and think he might have done better?' There is an honesty in this self-awareness which we can all relate to. Similarly, 'How can one of my grovelling class open a page of a standard author and not blush at his own stuff.' It was for this reason he could say to Lady Ossory, 'I hate to have anybody think better of me than I deserve' and mean it.

In the lengthy and perceptive pen-portrait which Mme du Deffand wrote of Horace in 1766 it is clear that she recognises this in him: 'it is obvious you are very intelligent in many ways,' she says and continues, 'You have absolutely no vanity although plenty of self-esteem; but your self-esteem does not blind you; it leads you to exaggerate your faults rather than to hide them. You give a good opinion of yourself only if forced to do so when comparing yourself with others.' Interestingly, she indulges in her own self-deprecation claiming, 'No one knows you less than I do', which is so absolutely not true, as she attributes this partly to Horace's 'inexcusable fear of ridicule.'

There is something paradoxical in what she has to say about Horace's friendships. 'Your friendship is steadfast,' she writes, and 'You have friends you are entirely devoted to.' Yet she adds, 'I cannot say anything about your dislike of friendship.' It is certainly true that Horace had friends he was devoted to. Twice he offered to bail out his cousin Henry Conway and most of the friendships he made at Eton lasted into his adult life, but he was by no means steadfast. The quarrel with Gray is a separate issue, but he fell out with Ashton, Montagu and Cole. The friendships which lasted longest were with those whom he rarely saw – Horace Mann for instance.

Horace was one of the most sociable of beings, but only when it suited him and that was not always. It has been said of him that he chose to be a spectator of life rather than participate in it. While still in his twenties he declared that his ideal existence would be if 'I had a house of my own in the country and could live there now and then alone.' Three years later he discovered Strawberry Hill, the perfect retreat. And when he travelled, as he did to visit the houses and gardens of the great, he preferred 'to travel without company, for then I take my own hours and my own humours.' There was something of the loner to him, even at times of the misogynist. John Chute received this outburst from Houghton.

> Oh, my dear Sir, don't you find that nine parts in ten of the world are of no use but to make you wish yourself with that tenth part. I am so far from growing used to mankind by living among them that my natural ferocity and wildness does but every day grow worse. They tire me, they fatigue me; I don't know what to do with them.

But paradoxical attitudes and behaviour are not uncommon qualities. As Henry James wrote after attending Robert Browning's funeral, 'A good many oddities and a good many great writers have been entombed in the Abbey; but none of the odd ones have been so great, and none of the great ones so odd.' And it is hard to equate the avant garde poet whose *Waste Land* so bewildered the world with the be-suited Eliot who, in his late twenties, posed outside Faber's offices, leaning on a rolled umbrella, wearing a bowler hat and, of all things, spats!

Paradox and contradiction are to be found everywhere in Horace's writings and in his life, and it is pointless to generalise or seek out some kind of synthesis. He told us a good deal about himself when he observed that, 'Life is a comedy to those who think and a tragedy to those who feel.' And in 1760 he wrote to George Montagu a long letter about the gout that had plagued him for years, 'Here I am lying upon a couch, wrapped up in flannels, with the gout in both feet.' And the complaints go on. We have heard them all before. But there is a PS. 'The gout has pinned me to my chair; think of Ariel the Sprite in a slit shoe!'

'Ariel the Sprite in a slit shoe'. We cannot be sure – I certainly cannot – exactly what it was he meant by that, but it seems so perfectly right.

One of the last letters he wrote – or rather dictated, as he could no longer hold a pen – was to Lady Ossory asking her not to show his 'idle notes' to other people, nor to praise them so. He wanted, he said, '...no more such laurels,' adding, 'I shall be quite content with a sprig of rosemary thrown after me, when the parson of the parish commits my dust to dust.'

There's rosemary, that's for remembrance.

BIBLIOGRAPHY

Primary Sources:

Walpole, Horace, *The Works,* 5 Volumes, Pickering & Chatto (London, 1999)

Walpole, Horace, *Memoirs and Portraits,* ed. Matthew Hoggart, Batsford, (London 1963)

Walpole, Horace, *Historic Doubts on the Life and Reign of King Richard III,* (London, 1768)

Walpole, Horace, *Hieroglyphic Tales,* Pallas Athene, (London, 2010)

Walpole, Horace, *The Castle of Otranto and The Murderous Mother,* ed. Frederick S. Frick, Broadview Press, (New York, 2011)

Walpole, Horace, *The Castle of Otranto and Hieroglyphic Tales,* ed. Robert Mack, Dent, (London, 1993)

Walpole, Horace, *Selected Letters,* ed. W.S. Lewis, (Yale, 1973)

Walpole, Horace, *Selected Letters,* ed. Stephen Clarke, Everyman, (London, 1926)

Bentley, Richard, *Designs by Mr Richard Bentley for six Poems by Mr T. Gray,* facsimile, Pallas Athene, (London, 2010)

Secondary Sources:

Anderson, Howard, *The Familiar Letter in the Eighteenth Century,* University of Kansas, (Kansas, 1968)

Brownell, Morris, *The Prime Minister of Taste*, (Yale, 2001)

Chalcraft, Anna, *Strawberry Hill,* Frances Lincoln Ltd. 2007.

Chase, Isabel, *Horace Walpole, Gardenist,* (Princeton, 1943)

Clark, Kenneth, *The Gothic Revival,* (London, 1928)

Curry, Neil, *William Shenstone,* (London, 2020)

Davoli, Sylvia, *The Lost Treasures of Strawberry Hill,* Scala Arts, (2019)

Fothergill, Brian, *The Strawberry Hill Set,* Faber, (London, 2009)

Frayling, Christopher, *Horace Walpole's Cat,* Thames & Hudson, London, 2009)

Greenwood, H.W., *Horace Walpole's World,* Bell & Son (London, 1913)

Groom, Nick, *The Gothic, A Very Short Introduction,* Oxford, (2012)

Gwynn, Stephen, *The Life of Horace Walpole,* (New York, 1932)

Haggerty, George, E., *Horace Walpole's Letters.* (Lewisburgh, 2011)

Harney, Marion, *Place-Making for the Imagination,* Routledge, (London, 2013)

Ketton-Cremer, R.W. *Horace Walpole,* Faber, (London, 1946)

Kallich, Martin, *Horace Walpole,* Twayne, (New York, 1971)

Lewis, W.S., *Horace Walpole, The Mellon Lectures,* Rupert Hart Davis, (London, 1961)

Mowl, Timothy, *Horace Walpole, The Great Outsider,* Faber, (London, 2010)

Munson, Aldrich Havens, *Horace Walpole and the Strawberry Hill Press, 1757-1789,* Kirkgate Press, (Pennsylvania. 1901)

Redford, Bruce, *The Converse of the Pen,* (Chicago, 1986)

Smith, Warren Hunter, *Horace Walpole, Writer, Politician and Connoisseur,* (Yale, 1967)

Strachey, Lytton, *Books and Characters,* (London, 1922)

Stuart, Dorothy Margaret, *Horace Walpole,* (Macmillan, (London, 1927)

White, T.H. *The Age of Scandal,* (London, 1950)

INDEX

Addison, Joseph *91,132-3*

Ashton, Thomas *14-18, 21-24, 31-35, 52, 82-83, 92,94, 254*

Baskerville, John *214*

Beauclerk, Lady Diana *122-124*

Bentley, Richard *63,64, 65, 72-75, 99-105, 113, 141, 231, 252*

Berry, Mary *39, 67, 70, 176*

Balmerino, Lord, *87-89*

Boswell, James *90, 122, 165, 266*

Bridgeman, Charles *46-47, 136*

Brown, Lancelot *138*

Burlington, Richard, 3rd Earl of *47, 57,122, 128, 132, 136-137*

Burney, Fanny *182*

Byng, Admiral *147-8, 160, 196-198*

Byron, Lord *183, 191*

Chatterton, Thomas *213-232*

Chenevix, Mrs *57*

Chesterfield, Philip, 4th Earl *193, 251*

Chute, John *34, 36, 44, 63, 64, 74-5, 81, 94, 139, 181, 231-2, 243, 254*

Clive, Kitty *77, 177, 190, 198, 243*

Cole, William *65-6, 118, 165, 167, 206, 232-238, 242, 254*

Coleridge, Samuel *182, 214, 235*

Collins, William *57, 250*

Conway, Henry *15, 24-6, 32, 36, 39, 40, 57, 68, 78, 124, 139-43, 154-157, 211, 224, 226, 229, 234, 238, 253*

Cowper, William *223, 224, 225, 249*

Cromartie, Lord *87*

Cromwell, Oliver *20, 68, 108, 251*

Damer, Anne *78,123-124, 127*

du Deffand, Mme *18, 73, 156, 166 173-174, 183, 188, 194, 206, 231, 238-240, 253*

Eliot, T.S. *187, 254*

Etheredge, George *20*

Fielding, Henry *57, 165, 171, 178, 207, 225, 250*

Gainsborough, Thomas *122, 125*

Garrick, David *77, 177, 200*

Gray, Thomas *12-18, 21-38, 81-83, 93-96, 98-108, 131, 162, 171, 182, 199, 216-217, 227, 231, 234-238, 243, 252-254*

Holland, Lord *10, 158*

Houghton Hall *39-56, 58, 61, 114, 116, 130, 136, 139, 145, 228, 237, 243, 254*

James, Henry *80*

Johnson, Samuel *38, 93, 98, 116, 122, 131-132, 162, 165, 174, 177, 193, 245*

Kent, William *46-49, 122, 136-137, 142*

Keats, John *213, 217*

Kirkgate, William *125-126*

Kilmarnock, Lord *87-88*

Kneller, Godfrey *50, 52, 114*

Lamb, Charles *235*

Lyttleton, Charles *13, 19, 44, 132*

Mann, Horace *11, 12, 29-30, 34-37, 40-45, 54-57, 62-68, 73, 77, 82-88, 93, 102-104, 108, 113, 120-126, 129, 137, 139-141, 145-151, 157, 162, 177, 179, 196, 198, 211, 224-231 241-243, 248-250*

Mason, William *14, 37, 75, 102, 120, 149, 206, 236-238, 250*

Macaulay, Thomas *109, 248-252*

McPherson, James *165, 215*

Middleton, Conyers *17-18, 31, 41, 83, 108, 250*

Milton, John *20, 135*

Montagu, George *13-16, 58, 63, 65, 67, 69, 76, 81, 86, 110-115, 138-142, 146, 156, 162, 181-182, 227-238, 242, 254-255*

Montagu, Mary Wortley, Lady, *10, 57*

Newcastle, Thomas 1st Earl of, *30, 85, 144, 149, 159, 197-198, 231*

Ossory, Countess *53-4, 122, 177, 208-211, 236, 238, 243-246, 253, 255*

Pope, Alexander *10, 20, 32, 47, 91-92, 102, 128, 131-133, 137, 162, 165, 178, 217, 224*

Richardson, Samuel *162, 171, 174, 178, 207-208, 250*

Ruskin, John *59, 213*

Scott, Walter *167, 179, 228*

Selwyn, George *157, 171*

Seward, Anne *221*

Shelley, Mary *175*

Shelley, Percy *266*

Shenstone, William *117, 130, 132, 244*

Sidney, Philip *20, 107-108*

Skerrett, Maria *9, 11, 22, 43*

Smart, Christopher *37*

Stephen, Leslie *163, 249*

Strachey, Lytton *12, 149, 250, 225-226, 266*

Strawberry Hill *17, 34, 40, 56-80, 97, 101, 104, 114, 120, 122-127, 139-142, 157, 161, 166, 170, 177, 183, 186, 199, 222, 233-244, 244-254*

Temple, William *135*

Thomson, James *57, 93, 108, 132*

Vertue George *114-116*

Voltaire *175, 197, 205*

Walpole, Lady *18*

Walpole, George, 3rd Earl *53-54*

Walpole, Horace

Works:

Aedes Walpolonianae *48-52, 146*

Anecdotes of painting *46, 115-123, 125, 129, 132, 216, 232*

Castle of Otranto *73-78, 161-180, 191, 201-207, 218, 235*

Catalogue of Royal and Noble Authors *105-111, 153, 249*

Description of Strawberry Hill *71-79*

Epistle from Florence *18, 31-33, 92*

Fugitive Pieces *113*

Hieroglyphic Tales *206-213*

Historic Doubts on the Life and Reign of Richard III *182, 199-206*

Letters *223-247*

Letter from Xo Ho *196-198*

Memoirs *147, 149, 154, 156-160, 249*

Mysterious Mother *122-123, 180-191, 239*

Reminiscences *246-247, 249*

Sermon on Painting *51-52*

West Richard *14-18, 22-28, 32-35, 47, 67, 93-94, 131*

Whitehead, William *61, 66*

Woolf, Virginia *125*

Wordsworth, William *213*

Young, Edward *115*